Smell the Bacon,
Charlie!

A CEO'S GUIDE TO IMPLEMENTING
ORGANIZATIONAL CHANGE

ROBERT J. HAWORTH

Smell the Bacon, Charlie! A CEO's Guide to Implementing Organizational Change, published January, 2022

Editorial and proofreading services: Highline Editorial, Katie Barger, Karen Grennan
Interior layout and cover design: Howard P. Johnson

Photo Credits:
Cover artwork by Layne Lundstrom, Out'a the linez
Interior illustrations by Layne Lundstrom, Out'a the linez
About the Author Photo: Owned by Robert J. Haworth

 **SDP Publishing**

Published by SDP Publishing, an imprint of SDP Publishing Solutions, LLC.

ISBN-13 (print): 978-1-7378019-1-7
ISBN-13 (ebook): 978-1-7378019-2-4

Library of Congress Control Number: 2021923522

Printed in the United States of America

TABLE OF CONTENTS

PREFACE 5

INTRODUCTION 7

Part I *Let's Tee This Up* 9

1 Change or Fail 11

2 What is Your "Culture for Change"? 17

3 The Change Model & the Players 25

4 It's All About People 47

Part II *Let's Get This Right* 49

5 Eggs & Bacon 51

6 The Burning Oil Platform: JUMP! 61

7 Let's Wash That Rental Car 67

8 Ready … Aim … FIRE! 81

9 Keep Your Eyes on the Prize 89

10 Pace: You Want It Done When? 95

11 Keep the Plane Flying 99

12 Celebrate, but Not for Too Long 103

13 Where's the Beef? Or, is That an Ugly "ROI Gap" I See Growing? 105

14 You're Right, It's Hard! 111

ACKNOWLEDGMENTS 113

ABOUT THE AUTHOR 117

PREFACE

This book begins a journey for me, and hopefully you, to identify and discuss one of the most important aspects of any successful business, which is moving the organization through a needed change to remain competitive in a rapidly changing business environment. The track record for successfully implementing change into an organization is, well, dismal. Depending on which book, or article, or journal one reads, the BEST success rate is 50 percent really.

Why do we need another book on organizational change? There are so many books written on this topic, and some are really good. There are textbooks that students use in business schools, and MBAs write papers and theses on this topic, but companies STILL keep screwing this up. You know what? I think that's unacceptable. So, this book is addressing this same topic, but in a new, and somewhat unconventional way. Any way you look at organizational change, it's hard. However, I believe the methods and concepts discussed in this book are the right ones to improve your odds of success.

This book is written as a guide for a CEO to use as he/she implements change in their organization. It is written in a somewhat discussion format to a CEO, whose name is Charlie. Why Charlie? Well, Charlie can be a man's name or a woman's name, and I like the name Charlie. Charlie is the CEO of a fictitious company, but a similar company to many of my clients over the years. Charlie runs a large, regional supermarket chain with around 500 stores.

I use a supermarket business in this book for two reasons. The first is because I love this industry. On the surface, it seems fairly simple and straightforward, but under the covers, it's highly complex with leading-edge technologies and razor-thin margins. The second is that—come on—everyone has been in a supermarket and understands the business model to some degree, so it's a great business to use as the example for the topics I will address in the book.

Although it's written to Charlie (the CEO), this book is for any executive or aspiring executive in any organization or industry (big, small, for profit, not-for-profit) who is involved in, or responsible for, a major project and wants to understand the right way to implement change successfully.

The first few chapters in the book introduce the concept of organizational change and the model that most organizations use to implement change, and I'm the first to admit, they're a bit boring. Sorry. The next nine chapters address those areas of organizational change that, well, you have to get right. As is stated earlier, not enough companies get this right, which is why I'm writing this book, so read on!

I hope this book contributes to your organization's success.

INTRODUCTION

Since this is my first book, let me introduce myself. I am one of the happiest and most fortunate persons I have ever met. The two main reasons for this good fortune are that I have a wonderful family, and I have had two amazing careers, so far.

My first career was approximately thirty years as a management consultant. Yes, I was one of those high-priced guys who borrows your watch and then tells you what time it is, and then of course sends you a bill! (More on consultants in Chapter 3.)

During the first two decades of my consulting career, I had the opportunity to work for three great global firms. Working for these firms, I was exposed to multiple industries and virtually every level within these organizations, as I would say "from the receiving dock to the board room." In addition, I was lucky to work with countless consulting colleagues who were, for the most part, smart and driven men and women.

When I turned forty, I believed I had the right level of experience and confidence to start and run my own firm. I put a business plan together, walked into work one day, and quit. I'll be frank, it was not a fun meeting. Over the next decade, I grew my business successfully, and we became recognized as the leading consulting firm in our area of specialization in the U.S. retail industry. We were always a small, boutique consulting firm, but we had an amazing team of women and men who were truly experts in their fields.

Over this thirty-year career, I was inside more companies and involved in more technology-driven client engagements than I can even remember.

After an amazing consulting career, I had the most wonderful second-career opportunity that any successful businessperson should consider. I became a college professor and taught in the classroom for seven years with incredible young adults. Over these seven years, I had the privilege of teaching my "kids" not only the fundamentals of strategy, management, and entrepreneurship, but also my real-world experiences, successes, and screw-ups. It was an amazing seven years and most certainly the highlight of my professional career.

Teaching is not only a great way to give back to the next generation of business executives, but it gives you time to think! Think about all those clients and all those projects. And yes, think about the book(s) you want to write.

Now I'm starting my third career as an author, where I can share my experiences, successes, and screw-ups with you. So, let's take this journey together and discuss the essential parts of business success.

Part I

LET'S TEE THIS UP

"IF YOU THINK YOU'RE GOING TO BE DOING BUSINESS IN TWO, THREE, OR FIVE YEARS THE SAME WAY YOU'RE DOING BUSINESS TODAY, WELL, THAT'S A GOING-OUT-OF-BUSINESS STRATEGY."

—ROBERT HAWORTH

1 Change or Fail

This is a concept that all CEOs should know, but let's tee this up. In today's dynamic, fast-paced, and highly competitive business environment, if you think you're going to be doing business in two, three, or five years the same way you're doing business today, well, that's a going-out-of-business strategy.

The title of this first chapter is "Change or Fail." What does it mean to "Fail"? Failure is a powerful word. In the context of this book, "to fail" ranges from:

✓ Failing to achieve your company's potential in the marketplace, such as losing market share to a competitor, or under-achieving in your profitability or return-on-invested-capital, to

✓ Going the way of Mervyn's, Radio Shack, Circuit City, etc.

As a college professor, it was fairly straightforward teaching students about management concepts, strategic planning models, and processes. What is so hard to teach in the classroom—and what students can't really learn until they experience it—is how competitive the business world is. One method I would use to try to drive home this point was to study and discuss companies that had achieved competitive advantage in their industry, only to lose their competitive position in a few short years. How could this happen?

What causes a company to fail? So many books and articles have been written on this topic (many of them very good), but in my opinion, it comes down to a CEO and executive team that either has *no* strategic vision and plan, or a *poor* strategic vision and plan, or a *poorly implemented* strategic vision and plan. Simple, right?

Although I do touch on strategic planning in this book, this book is not a guide to strategic planning. (That will be another book in the series.) It's a book about guiding your company through an organizational change that has been identified in your strategic vision and plan that is needed to stay competitive, to stay relevant in your industry, and ultimately, to stay in business and thrive.

The big question to ask is: What drives the need for an organization to change? Again, this is touching on some important steps in the strategic planning process, but let's all get on the same page about what drives change by looking at a few strategic planning models:

Fig. 1. External Environment

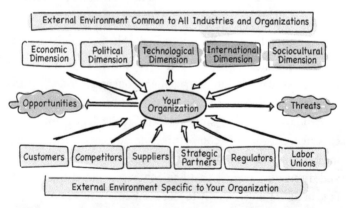

▲ *This diagram illustrates the major components of an organization's external environment that must be analyzed during the strategic planning process for potential opportunities and threats. It is certainly important to evaluate **current** opportunities and threats posed by these components, but for effective strategic planning, it is critical to determine **future** opportunities and threats based on forecasted or predicted changes occurring in these components.*

This is a similar diagram that I used to teach about the external environmental analysis component of strategic planning. I like this diagram because it's both simple and effective in identifying the areas of the environment that are possibly presenting both opportunities and threats to your industry and company. The top set of boxes on the diagram represent segments of the external environment that are common to all organizations and industries, but certainly impact your company: changes in technology; economic factors such as inflation, unemployment, and interest rates; changes in our society and culture; the ever-swinging pendulum of our political environment; and ever-dynamic international dimension. The bottom set of boxes on the diagram represent those aspects of the external environment that are specific to your industry and your company: your competitors, your customers, your suppliers, any strategic partners that your company works with, regulators that impact or influence your industry, and labor unions if they are present in your organization.

For any company in any industry, to be successful, sustainable, or even relevant over time, they need to clearly understand the components of their external environment, how these components are changing, and what those changes mean to the company's future strategic direction. The business world is littered with companies that failed to see changes coming in their customer demographics or sociographics, in new technologies, or in new and/or current competitors.

Porter's Model on Industry Forces

This classic strategy model helps companies understand external forces that are impacting their industry and company, and how these forces are changing and presenting either threats to their operations, or opportunities that should be seized.

Fig. 1.2 Porters's Five Forces Model

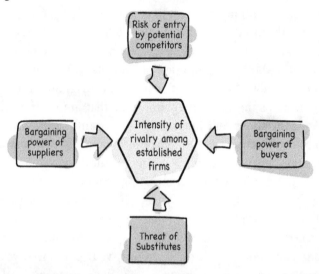

▲ *This famous strategy model, developed by Michael Porter, helps an organization evaluate the potential opportunities and threats posed by forces and dynamics that are occuring in its industry. Remember, it is important to evaluate the forces that are occuring today, but more importantly, it is critical to predict or forecast how these forces and dynamics are changing and evolving over your strategic planning horizon.*

Some brief examples—or questions—when looking at this powerful model include:

✓ Is there a risk of a new competitor entering our industry, perhaps one that is "disruptive" and may require us to rethink our business model (e.g. Amazon's massive impact on the retail industry)?

✓ Are our suppliers becoming more dependent on our company, and does this present the opportunity for us to negotiate/lower our costs, and negotiate better terms?

✓ Are our customers becoming more dependent on our company and its products, and does this present an opportunity to raise prices and increase our profitability? (Think about Intel and the computer industry's dependence on their products)

✓ Are our products becoming commodities and intensifying the competition in our industry based on pricing, which presents a significant threat to our future profitability unless we begin lowering our cost structure accordingly?

Over the years, a sixth box has been added to this model in some versions that addresses the "Power of Complementors." If your organization depends on complementors, such as application developers that add value to—or complement—your smart phone, you need to include this analysis in your strategic planning. Companies that fail to identify these basic threats or opportunities and fail to change their business models or strategies to address these external forces typically fail, or underperform.

Fig. 1.3 Competitive Advantage Model

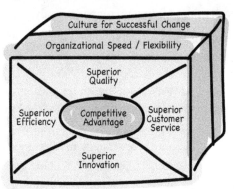

▲ *This strategy model helps an organization to evaluate the critically important questions of: How do we compete—or more importantly—how do we **plan** to compete in our industry to strive for competitive advantage? What internal strengths do we need to leverage, or what internal weaknesses do we need to fix in order to be successful in our chosen "go-to market strategy"? Is our current business model in alignment with this strategy?*

This simple, yet powerful, model addresses this strategic question: How does your company compete in the marketplace?

✓ Do we strive to gain competitive advantage through superior customer service, superior quality, superior pricing and efficiencies, or leading innovations?

✓ Does our company have superior speed or flexibility to bring products, solutions, or services to the market faster than your competitors?

✓ Does our company have a superior "culture for change" that enables it to successfully implement organizational change faster—or better—than your competitors?

✓ What is our company doing to either reach or sustain a superior position in the marketplace in the strategy you've chosen to compete in? How do we stack up to our competitors in these critical areas?

✓ Do we have the right technology systems in place to reach or maintain our competitive advantage?

✓ Is our business model in alignment with our strategies to excel in this area?

The list of strategy models goes on and on: the Industry Life Cycle; Distinctive Competency Model; Financial and Return-On-Invested-Capital (ROIC) Analysis Models.

But enough about these strategy models and the need for organizational change. Hopefully I've made the point that your company—and every company—is competing in a very dynamic world, and the pace of change is only increasing. I'm sure you know this already, Charlie.

Let's read on, Charlie, and discuss how to successfully implement organizational change into your business.

2 What Is Your "Culture for Change"?

"Your company's culture is the "soup" in which all activities take place." —Robert Haworth

Charlie, do you have the right company culture for change? It's an important question.

I initially wondered whether to give this topic its own chapter. I'll be the first to admit that I am not an expert on corporate culture, and there are so many other books focusing on this very important area of organizational management. This concept is so important that no change can ever be effective or long-lasting without understanding organizational culture. That is why this chapter is devoted to this essential question, and I'll ask it again: "What is your culture for change, Charlie?" Let's discuss.

It is popular today for companies to develop corporate culture edicts about things like: formal vs. casual attire, communications within the "chain of command" or the lack of "chain of command," open-work environments, who gets invited to meetings, titles or lack of titles, blah ... blah ... blah. It's one thing to *develop* the edicts, it's another thing to *live* the edicts.

The real corporate culture in any organization can be quite squishy. But let me stress, Charlie, that it is *so important* to have an open and conscious discussion about your corporate culture for change before embarking on any major change initiative, or even your strategic planning effort.

Let's discuss several of the most important aspects of your *culture for change* that will have the most profound impact on your organization's ability to successfully implement change. To be honest, whether your culture edicts include wearing Wingtips or Birkenstocks really doesn't matter when it comes to effective change.

What does matter includes:

- **Decision Making:** How does your company embrace decision making? In any business environment, decision making involves some aspect of risk. If a person or a team makes a decision that moves a project forward, but that decision turns out to be, well, not the best decision, how does your organization treat that person or team?

A STORY

I had a client in Dallas that was a large jewelry retailer. They had a somewhat toxic culture for decision making. If you made a decision that ended up to be a mistake, or if you made the wrong decision, you were singled out and punished, and everybody knew about it. How willing do you think people were to make decisions? I was the co-project manager on a large financial system implementation, and my counterpart was a fairly high-level manager in the Accounting Department. As the project was getting underway, it was obvious that this guy was not willing to make decisions that were needed to move the project forward. Big problem. I had to get the CFO involved with this situation where "assurances" were given to protect my co-project manager from persecution. Needless to say, this was a very difficult project. We finished the project successfully, but it was pretty ugly.

Are they punished, or is the approach: "Well, that was not the best decision and/or choice, so let's re-group, correct the decision, and move forward"?

- **Communications:** What is your culture for communication within your organization? How formal or informal does information get communicated up and down the chain-of-command? How does good news and bad news get communicated? Are you currently communicating to your organization through newsletters, website postings, and/or Facebook groups? Does your organization have an active and effective "grapevine" for communication? As we will discuss in future chapters, communication is a critical aspect for successful organizational change.

- **Politics:** I personally hate politics, and I really suck at playing political games. I think politics are a waste of corporate energy, and they typically never lead to positive outcomes for the common good. Remember, politics are all about "me," but politics are here to stay, like it or

A STORY

Okay, same jewelry retail client in Dallas. The politics were thick and toxic in this company. For example, the CIO and the CFO hated each other so much, they could barely be in the same room together. Not a situation for a smooth and successful implementation of a new financial system. How did we handle this? Well, being the "impartial outsider," I ended up being the "go-between" for the CFO and CIO. What did that mean? I got yelled at a lot (seriously ugly) because they couldn't yell at each other. As you might guess, we had some real fun project-status meetings. Good news: I survived.

not. Take a hard and honest look at the politics of your company. Successful organizational change requires cooperation between departments, executives, project teams, perhaps consulting firms, vendors, etc. How primed are your organizational politics for cooperation?

- **Management vs. employees relationship/trust:** Okay, let's state the obvious: Organizational change does *not* happen just at the management level, or just at the employee level. Successful organizational change happens across the entire organization, or division, or departments. It happens at all levels.

What relationship does your management level have with the employees? If you're sitting in the CEO's or senior executive's offices, this may be a difficult question to answer. What level of trust do the line employees have with management? Do they feel (in general) that management is looking out for their best interests, or do they feel management is always trying to screw them?

How have previous change initiatives/projects from the recent past been perceived by the line employees? Were any of these considered to be streamlining, cost-reduction, improved-efficiency projects where there were layoffs, jobs lost, or reduction of working hours? If so, there may be a (deserved) level of mistrust with your line employees on any future change initiatives. And we must be honest, many change initiatives are focused on those key areas of efficiency, streamlining, etc., and oftentimes there are employees who lose their jobs. That's reality in a highly competitive business environment.

Key questions for you to answer are: How were these layoffs or job losses handled? Did your line employees feel that their co-workers who lost their jobs were treated fairly, given severance, or assisted with job placement? Or was it just, "Adios," and "Don't let the door hit you on the way out"?

In my experience, line employees (and really all employees) in today's organizations both intellectually and emotionally understand that companies need to improve efficiencies to be competitive, and that people lose their jobs as part of those projects. Remember, it's always more important to treat the employees losing their jobs fairly for the employees who are staying. The group of employees who are staying after a layoff or a downsizing is the team that you need to move the company forward. If they feel their co-workers got screwed, well, they'll feel like the next time they will get screwed. Simple human behavior.

What is the management vs. employee situation in your company, Charlie? Do you have some challenges to address based on past sins, or do you feel your team of line employees has a good, trusting, professional work relationship with your management? You really must honestly address this question. Chapters 5, 6, and 7 address these important areas of management commitment, along with participation and ownership of the organizational change at all levels of the company. Pay attention here!

- **A Culture of Failure:** Past failures, or, "Why is this time going to be any different?" I have had clients in the past that literally had a culture of failure. And if you think about the fact that 50 percent of organizational changes do fail, it's not hard to understand this. I actually had a client in Portland, Oregon that had so many failed IT projects that there was a white-board on an easel outside the entrance to their IT development area that read, "At least the Titanic had a band." True story.

If your company, your team, or your employees have the attitude that your next project is going to fail just like the previous projects, well, that can't be good!

Charlie, after you and your team read this book, and you are preparing for a new and successful organizational change, you need to address this "culture of failure" issue honestly with your team ("Team, I have sinned!") and make them believe you are doing the right things this time to be successful. Easy, right?

I'll ask again, Charlie, how well is your organization's culture ready for change? Let's use the diagram on the following page (Figure 2.1) to discuss this concept. Diagram 2.1 is an

Fig. 2.1 Culture for Change Diagram

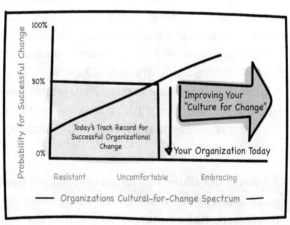

▲ *Use this simple diagram to discuss and evaluate where on the "Culture-for-Change Spectrum" your organization is today. What changes to your organization's culture can you make to improve your probability of success in implementing organizational change?*

over-simplified illustration of this very complex organizational culture assessment, but here's an important question: Where is your company on the spectrum for "culture for change"?

Honestly, Charlie, if your culture is leaning toward the "uncomfortable culture for change" side of the spectrum, to change your culture and move it in the direction of "an embracing culture for change" is really, really hard. Perhaps the hardest part of this will be *you looking in the mirror* and addressing your impact on this culture. It may also require changes at the senior-management level to get the right team "on the bus."

Now, I admitted that I am not an expert in corporate culture. If you believe that your organization's culture is not positioned for success on the "culture for change" spectrum, you should address this honestly and frankly with your management team and do one—or more—of the following:

- ✓ Read some books/articles on changing corporate culture.

- ✓ Hire a consulting firm specializing in corporate culture.

- ✓ Read this book at least once, and then buy a copy for everyone in your organization. (The second part of that recommendation perhaps benefits me more than you.)

- ✓ Do something.

Here is a good quote from a Harvard Business Review article on corporate change:

"Culture is like the wind. It is invisible, yet its effect can be seen and felt. When it is blowing in your direction, it makes for smooth sailing. When it is blowing against you, everything is more difficult."(*Changing Company Culture Requires a Movement, Not a Mandate* by Bryan Walker and Sarah A. Soule, June 20, 2017.)

Smooth sailing, Charlie!

3 The Change Model & the Players

I think it's important to level-set on what "implementing organizational change" is all about, at least from this book's perspective. I really don't want to get into the details, but a brief overview of what I'm talking about when I use terms such as organizational change, strategic initiatives, projects, and change initiatives, is appropriate, and hopefully will get all of us on the same page.

The business world is full of terms that have broad definitions and meanings. One of those terms is "organizational change." If you Google organizational change, you will get a myriad of websites and services that surround this critically important area of business management. But let's try to define it.

A couple of good definitions of organizational change and organizational change management come from a January 21, 2002 article by Tim Stobierski, from the Harvard Business School Online Business Insights Blog:

- **"Organizational change** refers to the actions in which a company or business alters a major component of its organization, such as its culture, the underlying technologies or infrastructure it uses to operate, or its internal processes."

- **"Organizational change management** is the method of leveraging change to bring about a successful resolution, and it typically includes three major phases: preparation, implementation, and follow-through."

I think these definitions are very much in line with this book and the concepts that I will discuss in chapters to come. If you read the definitions above one more time, they sound very straightforward and, well, sort of simple. But they are not. They are complex and very hard to get right.

Even if you read this book, and of course buy one for all of your employees (I need to try), and diligently follow all of my recommendations, successful organization change is still hard. Like I said in the introduction, Charlie, your company—and all companies—need to continually try to improve the change process and do what it takes to get this right. Anything else is unacceptable.

In the remainder of this chapter, I discuss the change model that is very typical across industries and organizations. In addition, I discuss "the players," or the people who are directly or indirectly involved in making this change happen in your organization. These players include internal departments and their employees along with external resources such as consulting firms, software companies, technology companies, etc.

If you are already familiar with a good organizational change model and the players involved in the change process, it won't hurt my feelings if you skim this chapter because I'm the first to admit it's a bit boring. But honestly, it's all important information for you to level-set the remainder of the book.

I'm including two diagrams (Figures 3.1 and 3.2) in this chapter to help explain this topic. Diagrams and pictures help cut through some of the jargon faster than explaining a complex process using academic terms that you may soon forget as soon as you turn the page. I hope these diagrams contribute to your better understanding of the topic.

Organizational Change Driven by Strategic Planning

As I discussed in a previous chapter, all organizations must change to survive. Change in well-managed companies is driven by some type of strategic planning process. Strategic planning is (and should be) different for organizations depending on: the size and complexity of the business; the size, complexity, and competitive dynamics of the company's industry; the stage of the business and its pace of growth; and the appropriate planning horizon for the business.

The diagram on the next page illustrates a fairly standard approach to strategic planning and how this planning process drives toward a Strategic Initiative or Project that the remainder of this book is all about. Let's walk through Figure 3.1 using the numbers in black circles to better understand the major steps in this process:

❶ REFERENCE TO FIG 3.1

Any effective strategic-planning process involves the analysis of both the external environment of a company as well as an in-depth analysis looking inside the business. A brief overview of this is as follows:

❶ **External Forces/Analysis:** Depending on your strategic-planning horizon, this look at the external environment is certainly looking at what is happening today, but more importantly, it's predicting changes in the environment over your planning horizon. Examples of these include:

- What changes in technology are occurring that will impact your business, your relationship with your customers, etc.?

Fig. 3.1 Strategic Planning Model

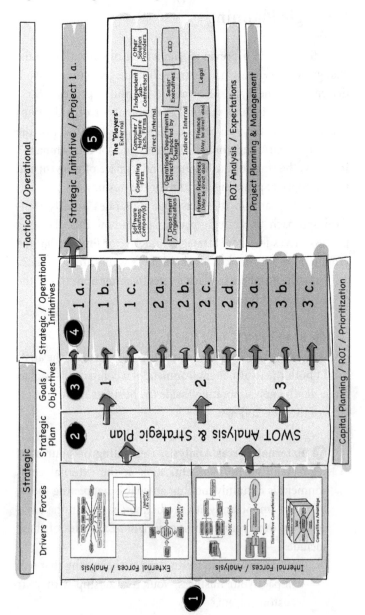

- How will predicted changes in the economy impact your business operations?

- Do you see a growing threat from one, or more, of your competitors?

- Do you see international companies entering your market and becoming competitive threats?

- Do you see the growth in your industry slowing and the intensity of rivalry growing between competitors in your industry?

- Do you see a new disruptive force occurring in your industry that may require significant changes to your business model?

❶ Internal Forces and Analysis: This part of strategic planning is all about taking a hard look inside your organization to identify both strengths and weaknesses. This is a hard thing for many companies to do without politics and hurt feelings kicking in and getting in the way. Imagine you are in an executive meeting to discuss internal weaknesses and problems, and sometimes the weaknesses and problems are *sitting at the table*. In companies with larger budgets, external consultants are often used for strategic planning, and this area of internal analysis is one where they can objectively look at internal performance and "say what needs to be said." Some examples of these include:

- What is your company's Return on Invested Capital (ROIC) both today, and projected into the future, and how does this stack up with your competitors?

◄ *This chapter is intended to get us all on the same page as to what "organizational change" is all about, and this diagram shows how the strategic goals and objectives lead to the tactical development of a strategic initiative or project. Implementing this strategic initiative into your organization is the "organizational change" that this book is all about. Are we on the same page?*

Who is gaining/losing the financial advantage in your industry?

- Depending on how your company competes in your industry (on pricing, on quality, on service, etc.), how are you performing against your competitors? How are the dynamics in these areas predicted to change over your planning horizon?

- Has your company gained any "distinctive competencies" in your industry, and how can you capitalize on these?

- On the flip side, do you have competitors gaining distinctive competencies, and what are you doing about it?

❷ REFERENCE TO FIG 3.1

Based on the results of the external and internal analysis, most companies develop some type of SWOT analysis documenting their Strengths, Weaknesses, Opportunities and Threats. The next big question is: "So what?" What is your company going to do about these SWOTs, which leads to the development of strategic goals and objectives?

Let's discuss an example of a possible SWOT analysis, then identify a Strategic Goal/Objective that would address this "So what?" Let's use your company for this example, Charlie.

✓ Based on the internal analysis of your financial performance, you have identified a weakness in your current and projected ROIC compared with several of your closest competitors. Drilling down into the ROIC analysis, you have identified that your Return on Sales has been sub-par and is projected to remain that way unless store operating costs are lowered.

✓ Your external analysis has identified several competi-

tors using new technologies in their store workforce
management area, thus lowering their overall costs of
store operations.

❸ REFERENCE TO FIG 3.1

Your company sets a strategic goal/objective to *lower store
operating costs by 3 percent over the next three years*, while
maintaining current levels of customer service in the stores.
In Figure 3.1, this would be Goal/Objective #1. Good strategic
goal and objective, Charlie!

❹ REFERENCE TO FIG 3.1

Based on your company's goal of lowering operating costs
by 3 percent over the next three years, you have identified
three *Operational Initiatives* that will need to be successfully
implemented in order to achieve this goal.

Let's work through an example for this retailer and say
that the three Operational Initiatives identified in your strategic plan in order to achieve Goal #1 are:

- ✓ **1a.** the implementation of a new store-wide workforce
management system and set of processes to lower labor
costs (e.g. reduce wasted labor) while maintaining (or
possibly increasing) current customer service levels;

- ✓ **1b.** the implementation of a new store-shrink management system in order to reduce inventory losses and
write-offs; and

- ✓ **1c.** the implementation of a new front-end configuration and installation/upgrade of your current Point-of-
Sale system to improve productivity (e.g. lower costs) of
your front-end labor.

As part of the strategic-planning process, the high-level
estimated costs/benefits of each of these initiatives and their
related Return-on-Investments (ROI) are created for review by

the capital committee/senior executive/etc. for approval of the final strategic plan. The type of ROI analysis performed at this step depends on the company, and it can take the form of ROI percent, net present value (NPV), internal rate of return (IRR), break-even analysis, etc. Regardless of the method used by your company, the idea is to determine the impact these initiatives will have on your company's performance and which initiatives have the potential for the largest impact.

Based on this ROI analysis, the Operational Initiatives are approved (or rejected) and then prioritized.

This can be, and often is, the conclusion of the strategic planning process. Way to go, Charlie!

I know that this was a major over-simplification of strategic planning. But hopefully it has provided a general framework for all of us as we now start discussing the focus of the remainder of this book, which is the successful achievement of change in your organization by successfully implementing Operational Initiatives, Projects, or whatever other name your company calls these important initiatives that are so critical to get right to maintain your competitive position in your industry.

❺ REFERENCE TO FIG 3.1

As Figure 3.1 vividly illustrates, this Operational Initiative 1a now becomes a real project, with real resources assigned to it, with real work plans and completion dates, and a real ROI that is expected to be achieved once this project is *successfully* completed.

The final step is to put together the project team to get this done. The section below looks at this team and the various players involved in this important change-process for your company.

It may seem painless on paper, but in reality, these decisions are make or break for many organizations and can affect the livelihoods of thousands of employees and management.

The Players in the Organizational Change Process

Full disclosure, for almost three decades, I was a player in this Organizational Change Model. Please forgive me, for I have sinned!

Typically, when an organization sets out to implement an operational initiative, they put together a team that is represented by both external and internal players. Figure 3.2 illustrates this set of potential players who could be—and often are—involved in these projects.

A very important consideration to discuss when looking across this team of players is: Who is *accountable* for achieving the ROI that the business expects from this initiative? We will re-visit this topic again later in the chapter.

Let's briefly discuss the players and their roles in this project:

Fig. 3.2 The Players in Organizational Change

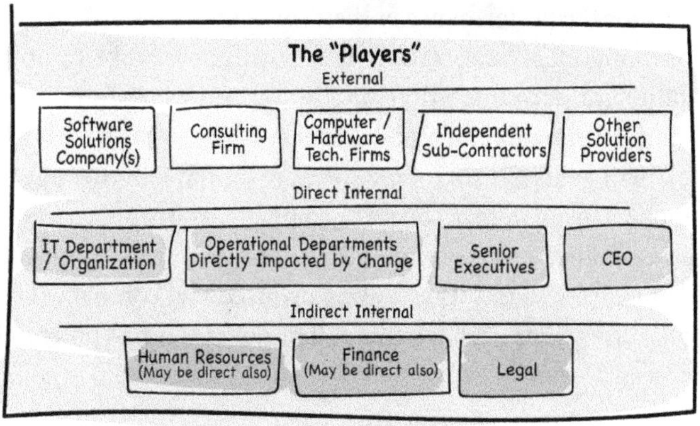

▲ *This diagram illustrates both the external and internal players involved in the implementation of an organizational change initiative. Another important message in this chapter is: Out of the 12 groups of players (the boxes), how many are ACCOUNTABLE for the benefits that the organization will expect from this change initiative?*

External Players

Software Solution Company(s)

These companies play a critically important role in organizational change. Across any industry—and any functional area within that industry—you will find companies providing software and technology solutions for those areas of the business. These companies often bring leading-edge technology and functionality to the clients and industries they serve.

Once the promises are made, and the sale is complete, these companies may or may not be involved in the implementation of their solution into your business. This often depends on size of the software company, their business model, and the relationship they have with implementation firms such as consulting firms, which we will discuss next. In fact, my company was one of these consulting firms that partnered with software solution providers to implement their software into our clients' organizations.

These software companies will most likely take responsibility for the performance of their software (as promised), but you can almost be certain that they will never take responsibility (or accountability) for the success of your project, and the ultimate return on investment (ROI) that your business will achieve using their software. Sorry, Charlie, but to be fair, if you were a software company, you wouldn't take responsibility or accountability for any ROI from a project. There are too many other players involved that could mess up and cause the project to either fail or not achieve its potential success.

Consulting Firm(s)

Not all companies use consulting firms to help them implement operational initiatives into their business. However, for companies with larger projects—and more complex and risky projects—the use of a consulting firm to help them implement these strategic and operational initiatives is common.

Remember, I was one of these consultants for almost thirty years, so I may be a bit biased here, but I believe that consulting firms have driven a significant amount of leading-edge thinking and revolutionary change into the business environment in the past forty years.

The role that consulting firms typically play in the implementation of these operational initiatives includes expertise with the software solution, expertise in the industry or functional area being impacted by the project, and the ability to bring a number of resources to the project, including smart and capable people. These consultants can fill the temporary spike of needed resources during the duration of these projects.

However, it's important to say that when engaging a consulting firm to assist your company with an operational initiative, it's essential to hire the right firm and manage them effectively. Certainly a topic for another book.

Never forget, Charlie, this is *your* project, not the consulting firm's project. Some of the biggest project failures that I have seen in my career were when the company/client abdicated responsibility of the project to their consulting firm, which typically results in "consultants-run-amuck" where nobody inside the company takes the needed ownership to make the implementation of the software, technology, changed processes, or whatever the organizational change is, successful. Really! (Sidebar: I'm happy to report that none of those failed projects were ones I was involved with.)

An important and final note on consulting firms as players in this organizational change model is that it is very rare that a consulting firm will take responsibility or accountability for the overall success and ROI attainment for a project. Again, too risky! These consulting firms are certainly held account-able for their performance—most likely the performance and progress of the project and its deliverables—but rarely are they held accountable for the eventual achievement of the ROI that was used to sell the project.

It's important to discuss the situation where the organiza-tion undergoing this change has outsourced their IT function to a consulting firm or another outside technology company. Let's clearly make the distinction that "outsourcing" is not "consulting." They are completely different. I should also say that I have never been a proponent of outsourcing IT. You may disagree with me, but I've never seen the relation-ship between the outsourcing firm and the company go well. However, when IT is outsourced, the role that the outsourcing firm plays in the organizational change model will vary by the terms of the outsourcing contract. So, for this book, let's assume that the role of the outsourcing firm in the change-management model will be similar (enough) with the internal IT organization discussion below.

Computer/Hardware Technology Firms

Again, the role these companies play in a project is very depen-dent on the type of operational initiative being implemented. These companies provide products/services that include servers, networks, cloud services, computer hardware, etc.

Typically, once the contracts are signed and the tech-nology is installed or available for use, the role these types of companies play in the overall project is limited, except for the on-going support and maintenance of their technology solutions.

Independent Sub-Contractors

Today, it is very common for companies to use indepen-dent sub-contractors to staff projects and day-to-day work, particularly in Information Technology departments/organizations within a company. These sub-contractors can work for either themselves, or for a company that staffs out these resources to their clients for a certain amount of time. These sub-contractors are often men and women who show up for work every day at their client and sit right next to employees of their client, oftentimes doing the same work as the employees but not getting any company benefits (e.g. health insurance, 401k's, paid vacation, etc.). On large operational initiatives like those we are focusing on in this book, it is very common to have sub-contractors performing some of the project tasks. These sub-contractors can be hired directly by the company through a sub-contracting firm or through your consulting firm. Regardless of who has hired these players, they will never be accountable for any ROI of a project. They will only be accountable for the work that they have been hired to do.

Other Solution Providers

Depending on the type of project being performed, there may be other solution providers that are hired to assist with a project.

These players can include architectural firms, engineering firms, law firms, etc. They typically have a very specialized role in the project and certainly will *not* be accountable for any ROI. *Is there a theme building here?*

Internal Players

Internal players are employees of your company who are staffed on this specific operational initiative. These players can either be directly involved in the project—perhaps being assigned on a full-time basis—or indirectly involved and providing service, input, and guidance on an as-needed basis. Let's discuss this important group of players.

Direct Internal

IT Department/Organization: The Information Technology or Information Services organization and/or department within a company (the name may vary across organizations) typically selects, implements, and supports all of the technology solutions across areas of the organization. Once a strategic initiative is established and it becomes a project, the IT Department typically remains heavily involved as a key player in the process. In addition to the hands-on technical role of a project, the IT Department often provides other services such as project management, training, and vendor management.

With these ideas in mind, I'm going to make some statements and observation about IT organizations that you may disagree with or may not apply to your specific organization.

During my career of working with clients to perform these projects, there is no question that for the majority of the projects, the IT organization was the primary initiator or driver of the change.

What I mean by this is that the IT organization—either through the strategic planning process or some type of reactive change (discussed in Chapter 1)—is the one identifying the need for change and bringing the potential solutions for this change to senior management. There are certainly good and valid reasons that IT is the initiator of these changes. They are more often the ones keeping up with new technologies, software, and capabilities in the marketplace, and they are also more aware of the limitations, cost of maintenance, and ownership of the organization's current systems. All of these factors are important and value-added for their organization, especially in the rapidly changing technology environment that we live in today. Let's not forget, however, that IT organizations sometimes need to substantiate their existence in the organization by always having the next best solution in their project pipeline, and let's be honest, they really like working on the latest and greatest technologies!

When IT is the driver of these change initiatives, it can be a classic good news versus bad news situation. The good news is that all organizations need to be aware of new opportunities to improve their operations and become more competitive, and IT organizations are often the ones leading the charge on identifying these new opportunities. I believe this is one very important role that IT organizations play.

Now let's discuss the bad news, which is something I've seen in far too many clients over the years, and that is the "IT shoving it down our throats" syndrome.

To be fair and honest, this is not an IT problem, it's a senior management problem that we will discuss later in Chapters 5, 6, and 7. The syndrome of IT pushing new technologies on the organization and the workplace resisting the change required to implement this new technology was a fairly common occurrence with my clients during my career. The following story of one of my clients is a great example.

A final point on IT organizations and their roles as players in organizational change. It is very rare that IT departments are held accountable for the ROI of a project, and probably rightly so. Even though the IT team is very involved in the ROI calculation that is used to sell and approve the change initiative, once the team performs and completes the key roles that it plays on a project, it typically becomes the responsibility of the operational department to deliver the ROI to the business. Let's discuss these operational departments.

We have just discussed six major players in the organizational change model and NONE of them is accountable for the ROI benefits that the business is expecting from this organizational change. Very interesting!

A STORY

My consulting company was hired by a very large regional drug store retailer to assist them with the implementation of a new workforce management system. Shortly after we were engaged and the project was getting underway, we learned that this project was initiated and being driven by the CIO of the company. The CIO was well known in the industry as a leading-edge technology thinker and was a very influential and convincing executive with other members of the senior management team, especially the CEO. The senior vice president of Store Operations was a bit "old school" and believed their current workforce management system in the stores was working well and did not need replacing. He clearly felt this new system was being shoved down his throat by the "hot shot" CIO.

You can probably guess how the project proceeded. The store operations team (you know, the ones who would be using this new system in their stores every day) never took ownership of this project and resisted its progress from the start. The project was not going well (anyone surprised?) and the CIO, sensing a pending disaster that would tarnish his reputation, suddenly and somewhat quietly shut the project down. Another failure? Well, everyone seemed to be happy with this decision except for me. I had to go find another client. Crap!

Operational Department(s) Directly Impacted by the Change: To be clear, when I say "operational department" I'm referring to the operational/functional part of the business directly being impacted by this change. This could be Manufacturing, Distribution, Retail Operations, Banking Operations, Accounting, Sales, Marketing, etc. depending on the company and its industry.

Using our retail workforce management example, the operational department for that change initiative would be the Retail Store Operations organization, including store employees, store management teams, district managers, regional managers, and on up to the senior vice president of Retail Operations.

This operational group will be the one using this new system and processes on a day-to-day basis in the business. We will discuss the senior executives next, but this operational department is generally expected to deliver the benefits to the business from this change. Since most of the discussions in future chapters will be focusing on this operational group, let's move on.

Senior Executives: These men and women are the members of the executive management team who are responsible and accountable for a major part/division or functional area of the business. Depending on the organization, these senior executives can either be the "chiefs" (chief financial officer, chief operating officer, chief information officer, etc.) or senior vice presidents, or vice presidents, or a combination of all three. But you get the idea, right? These are important men and women who are responsible for running a major part of the business or organization.

For example, in my consulting experience, the senior vice president of Store Operations was most typically my direct client and the person who was primarily responsible for the projects that my firm was hired to work on.

As we move through the players of organizational change, remember we are not only discussing their roles in this process, but we are also trying to determine *who* is going to be accountable for the organization achieving the benefits and ROI of this organizational change. One would assume that the senior executive of the operational area involved in this project or initiative would be the primary player to take both the responsibility and accountability for the ROI expected from this change. But, not so fast.

This was a meeting I'll never forget. Though I can't

A STORY

One of my more interesting clients in Dallas was the country's leading computer and software superstore. My firm was hired to assist them with the implementation of a chain-wide inventory management system that linked store-level and distribution center inventory across the chain. This type of inventory management is common today, but at the time, these systems, processes, and technologies were fairly new and risky to implement. A colleague of mine and I were sitting in the CFO's office to discuss the final contracts and plans for the project. This CFO had been recently hired by this retailer to help them with the explosive growth in stores they were experiencing. Toward the end of our contract discussion, he reached under his desk and pushed a "secret" button. The door to his office closed by itself (really). Of course, I was thinking to myself, "Now this should be interesting." He then proceeded to tell us that the reason he was hiring our firm to assist him with this project was that his previous company had just tried to implement a similar system. The project failed miserably and the executive in charge of that project was fired. He then told us that he was hiring us because he didn't want to get fired at the end of this project. Wow, very interesting. This senior executive had just pushed all of his responsibility and accountability for this risky project onto us, his consultants.

remember all of the senior executive clients I worked with on projects during my thirty-year career, I do remember that only a handful of executives took responsibility and accountability for their change initiatives and were truly committed to achieving the benefits for their businesses.

The rest, it seems, can be grouped into one or more of the following syndromes:

- ✓ The senior executive who feels that this change initiative is being shoved down their throat by the IT Department, and they are *not* going to take sole responsibility for this project, or;

- ✓ The senior executive who is new to the job and "inherited" the change initiative from their predecessor. This typically results in the "this was not my idea" syndrome, or;

- ✓ The senior executive (like the CFO in the story above) who wants to cover their you-know-what by hiring a consulting firm to take the risk and the blame for a possible failed project.

So, Charlie, what are your senior executives like?

Is anyone in the building going to take responsibility and accountability for this organizational change?

CEO: Well, that's you, Charlie.

In this book, I will make the point over and over again that the CEO is the single most important person in moving an organization through a major change. Certainly, the CEO is not involved in projects on a day-to-day basis—not even close—but he or she is the one person in the company who has the ultimate responsibility and accountability for moving their company through the needed changes to keep the company competitive and profitable.

My recommendation for the CEO's role in these projects—your role, Charlie—will be discussed in almost every chapter to follow, so let's leave these discussions for later.

Indirect Internal

These are organizations within your company that may get involved with a project or provide service and/or advice to a project, depending on the area of the business being addressed in this change.

Some examples include:

- ✓ **Human Resources:** If projects involve re-assigning people in the organization to work on project teams, or hiring people or sub-contractors to work on projects, or laying off employees as a result of projects, the Human Resource Department can and usually does play an indirect, but key role on many projects.

- ✓ **Finance/Accounting:** Somebody's got to pay for this, right? But seriously, the Finance/Accounting Department usually is involved with the development and/or approval of any project ROI that is used to justify project costs. Again, indirect, but very important on any project.

- ✓ **Legal:** Most projects involve contracts with software companies, consulting firms, technology companies, etc., and will need some type of assistance from your legal department or from an external law firm. Also, if labor unions are involved or impacted by a project, your legal department may play an indirect, but key role.

- ✓ Depending on the project and its impact on the business, other organizations within your company may be involved and play a key supporting role.

So, that's the change model and the players. Are we all on the same page? Good.

The next chapter will be very short, but the message is important and powerful.

Let's keep moving.

4 "It's All About People"

Success or failure in implementing organizational change is all about people, not technology.

Yes, there are problems with technology that can put a project at risk, and yes, there are software/technology vendors that "mislead" their customers or bring products to market that are not ready-for-prime-time but those problems can be solved. However, when people-problems occur during organizational change, which can include people's resistance to change, political challenges, cultural challenges, human resource challenges, and executive commitment problems, the likelihood of success is, well, dismal.

We will be discussing many of these people-issues throughout the book, and we've already addressed some in this chapter. But let's list a few of the more common:

✓ People generally hate change!

✓ Lack of ownership in the change.

✓ "You're shoving this down my throat!"

✓ "This may be your project, Charlie, but it's not my project!"

✓ Threatened self-interests.

✓ "How will this affect my job?"

✓ "Will I lose my job?"

- ✓ Lack of understanding: Why do we need to be making this change?

- ✓ "What's wrong with our current system and process? Politics, stinky politics."

- ✓ "What's in it for me?"

So, right out of the gate we need to get the people-issues and challenges right!

A lot of information to ponder in a very short chapter.

This wraps up the "Let's Tee This Up" section. Now let's move into the meat of the book and "Let's Get This Right."

Part II

LET'S GET THIS RIGHT

"CHARLIE, THE BUSINESS WORLD IS LITTERED WITH FAILED ORGANIZATIONS THAT COULDN'T GET THIS STUFF RIGHT."

—ROBERT HAWORTH

CHAPTER

5 Eggs & Bacon

I know you're busy, Charlie. A CEO's plate is usually full, and it's critical you manage your time effectively. CEOs are important men and women who have the most influence on their organization's success or failure.

In my opinion, the most important job of any CEO is to ensure his or her company gains competitive advantage, or at a minimum, stays competitive in a highly competitive and rapidly moving business environment. What that means is the CEO's primary job is to successfully lead their organization through the needed changes to maintain competitiveness.

Throughout this book, we will discuss over and over again how hard change is for an organization to implement successfully. In a previous chapter, we learned that "it's all about people," and generally speaking, people hate—and will resist—change. And no, I'm not talking about people just at the lower levels of the organization. I'm talking about people at *all* levels of the organization, including executives.

Let's say, Charlie, that you have done a great job to this point in putting together the right team of consultants, vendors, your IT and operations personnel, your steering committee, and other supporting resources. You've done a great job of convincing your organization that the "oil platform is on fire" (Chapter 6), and now they understand why this change is taking place and the fact that the company needs to move forward. But Charlie, change is still hard.

In addition to these people-challenges, let's don't forget about the other challenges that can impact a successful implementation, such as technology problems, budget issues, timing issues, and all of those day-to-day issues and problems of running your business. So, what does it take?

In my opinion, the number one requirement for an organization to successfully implement change is a *committed senior executive*. No, not a CEO or senior executive who has taken responsibility for the change (project). I mean a CEO or senior executive who is *committed*. What do I mean by commitment?

Here is an illustrated joke about the huge difference between being responsible and being committed. Perhaps not a great joke, but a joke nonetheless.

It is critically important, Charlie, for your organization to know that you and your executive team are committed to this change and see actions from you that demonstrate this commitment. Commitment to make the tough decisions, to

Fig. 5.1 Bacon and Eggs Joke Drawing

In a Bacon & Eggs Breakfast...

The chicken was responsible, but the pig was committed!

▲ *This is a good joke to remember the difference between an executive who is responsible versus one who is committed. Big difference!*

spend the money, to break down barriers and roadblocks, to assign the right personnel to the project (discussed more in Chapter 7), and to lead your organization successfully through this tough change.

In almost thirty years of working with clients to implement change into their organizations, how many CEOs were involved and truly committed? In every project that I was involved with in my career, there was a senior executive or some level of vice president who was assigned responsibility for the project. This person was the project "executive sponsor" and was the executive we expected to deal with for project planning, status tracking, issue resolution, and, of course, to pay our invoices! Honestly, these senior executives ran the gambit from those who took their responsibility seriously and did show commitment, to those who clearly demonstrated they felt this project was being forced upon them and their organization by IT, the consulting firm, or the CEO.

So, back to my question: How many CEOs were involved with my projects and truly demonstrated commitment? None whom I can remember. Oh yeah, I remember there was one. . . .

A STORY

One of the most interesting projects of my career involved working with a national supermarket and drug company to implement a new strategy and technology for workforce management within store operations. The company had set a strategic direction to move from a "holding company" where each major food or drug division operated somewhat autonomously, to an operating company with common systems, processes, etc. The driving force of this change was to operate more efficiently and effectively as a larger organization in order to be more successful in an industry being "disrupted" by Walmart. (continued)

A STORY

Our project was one of many that the company had going on simultaneously. My firm was hired to assist this company in the selection and implementation of new labor management software, along with the development and integration of engineered labor standards and processes for all store departments. Great project.

On this project, I had the opportunity to work with the best client executive I had ever worked with in my career. This executive had been the senior vice president of Operations for one of the major divisions of this company, and he'd been brought into the corporate organization to take responsibility for several key store operation projects. This executive was smart, experienced, and well respected within the organization. The challenge was that he was limited in his power over the executives running the various divisions of company, some of whom had not bought into this new vision and direction of the company. That power resided in the CEO and a handful of senior executives at the corporate level of the company.

I knew this was going to be a difficult project. We were implementing new technologies and processes into hundreds of stores in a very large and complex organization, which is always tough. But then, there was the political environment that I knew would present significant roadblocks. Each of these divisions had their own technologies (and their related organizations) that were being replaced or consolidated into the corporate operation. As you can imagine, there was much uncertainty and resistance from these organizations within the divisions. Remember, it's all about people.

(continued)

A STORY

For the big kickoff meeting for this project, I recommended to my client executive that he invite the CEO to open this meeting with a clear discussion of his vision, how this important project fit into this vision, and how he strongly believed that if his team of division executives weren't "on the train with him to implement this vision" then they should get off the train now! The CEO agreed to play this role at our kickoff meeting, and he did a great job in delivering this message. Great, right? Well, the problem was that this was the last time we saw the CEO.

In our next major meeting, we had the various workforce management teams and operational executives from each division come to the corporate office to review the upcoming project in detail. We discussed the new systems, engineered labor standards, new processes, and anticipated benefits and operating improvement. During this meeting, one of the senior vice presidents of Operations for one of the major divisions tried to sabotage the meeting and project. Behind the scenes (actually in the bar at the hotel the night before the meeting), he was turning the key workforce management teams from each division against this project and encouraged them to resist this change. The next morning, the meeting was ugly. Despite the growing headwinds, the project proceeded, but it was an on-going struggle.

We never did determine why this senior vice president was trying to sabotage the project, but if I was a betting man, I would put my money on him feeling threatened by this new system and the overall vision of consolidation. He was going to lose some of his responsibility for

(continued)

A STORY

a very important function in his stores: the scheduling and management of store labor. As you might guess, the workforce management teams from the various divisions that we were working with knew that their boss didn't support this new initiative, so how supportive do you think they were? This was an on-going challenge with this project, and unfortunately, the CEO never stepped in to correct this problem.

This project, along with all of the projects underway to implement this new vision, was never completed. This major national supermarket and drug company was acquired by another major supermarket and drug company, and the project was shut down. (The situation that led to this acquisition is discussed in Chapter 11.) So, one more failed change implementation!

To be fair to the CEOs of my clients over the years, they may have been more involved in projects behind the scenes. I was a consultant and not invited to all internal meetings where the CEO may have been in attendance and involved in the process. But I was in all of the status meetings and all of the steering committee meetings, and I have no memory of any CEOs being actively involved—and more importantly, showing commitment—in any of those meetings. They were not visible to the project team and the internal and external players who were getting this change initiate done. Unfortunately, not many demonstrated commitment.

What do I mean when I say that your people need to see "actions" that demonstrate your commitment? I certainly understand that, as CEO, you have a lot on your plate, and there is only so much time you can commit to this project.

Let's discuss some areas where a CEO needs to be involved and is demonstrating all-in commitment.

- **Strategic Planning:** Hopefully, Charlie, the need for this project was identified in your organization's strategic planning process and is clearly tied to one or more of the **S**trengths, **W**eaknesses, **O**pportunities, or **T**hreats (SWOTs). Certainly, as CEO, you were intimately involved in this strategy development, and therefore approved this project as part of the execution of your strategic plan. In addition, you must show leadership and commitment, as key managers eventually "work" the SWOT elements.

- **Project Capital Funding:** If your organization is like most, this project was reviewed and approved by some capital committee. If not a member of this committee, Charlie, you certainly need to be a regular participant.

  Typically, some team has developed an ROI analysis for this project showing business benefits versus costs, which the capital committee has reviewed and approved. This team can consist of operational, financial, and technology people from your organization, and perhaps a group of outside consultants.

  It is critical that CEOs are involved at key points during this capital funding process. It is imperative that they clearly understand—and agree with—the ROI analysis, and that, as a leader, they clearly assign one of your executives to take *responsibility* and *accountability* in achieving this ROI. This executive should represent the operational area impacted by this project and should be as committed to the success of the project as the CEO.

- **Project Planning & Organization:** Most likely, the team that put together the detailed ROI analysis will be tasked with the initial planning of the project and the development of the project organization and its key members.

In Chapters 3 and 7, I address the composition of this project organization and its importance for the success of this effort. This is a critical time for you to demonstrate your commitment to this change by making the tough decisions required to put the right team together for this project. Your involvement during this step will have a long-range impact on the success of the project.

Typically, during this project planning and organization step, a steering committee will be formed to oversee the project and provide executive oversight and guidance to the project team. The steering committee is usually comprised of the key executives from the business that are impacted or directly involved in this change, along with other executives who can provide valuable insight for the team, such as Human Resources, Finance, and Legal, depending on the areas this change will be impacting. And yes, the CEO should be either an active member, or at a minimum, an active participant in the steering committee. Think about it, if you are not actively involved in this steering committee, how can you be demonstrating your commitment to the success of this effort?

- **Project Execution & Tracking:** As the project team proceeds with the execution and implementation of this change, your involvement will decrease significantly. Depending on the duration of the project, the team will typically conduct steering committee meetings either monthly, quarterly, or at key milestones in the project. The culture of this steering committee should be one of: "What can we, as a group of executives, do to help your team be successful?"

During these meetings, the project team, at a minimum, reports status against the plan, discusses problems and issues that need resolving, and presents the projected outlook for the project over some time horizon.

The steering committee's job is to make needed decisions, provide guidance, discuss possible scope changes to the project (see Chapter 9), and break down any roadblocks the team may have toward making progress. On paper, it looks pretty easy, right?

The following statement is a universal truth: "Change is tough, and projects don't always go as planned." Unfortunately, too many steering committee meetings take the "low road" and end up being witch hunts, blame games, "I told you so's," and political battlegrounds. Don't let that happen, Charlie. In my experience, those projects don't end well!

Your time commitment during this step of the project is minimal, but the commitment you demonstrate during this step is critical to the project's success.

- **Project Completion and Metrics Accountability:** Chapter 13 is dedicated to this topic, so I won't spend much time here discussing it, but I'll remind everyone to not forget about that ROI.

  After the project is complete, your role, along with the senior executive to whom you initially assigned responsibility and accountability for the results, is to ensure that the business benefits from the project are being measured and achieved. It is simply amazing (or pathetic) how seldom this step takes place after a major change initiative in an organization. Again, see Chapter 13.

Charlie, now you know that your commitment is essential for successfully implementing organization change into your company. Smell the bacon, Charlie! As you well know, it takes more than a committed CEO to implement change. It takes an organization that clearly understands *why* this change is needed and is ready to move forward with you to make it happen. This leads us to our next chapter.

CHAPTER

6 The Burning Oil Platform: JUMP!

People generally hate change. They're comfortable in their current environment, with their current systems and procedures, and change presents risk, uncertainty, and fear. But you already know that, Charlie.

When an organization enters a period of crisis, people within the organization typically know it. When sales are down, or market share is being lost to competitors, or the company has been losing money, or layoffs are occurring, it is much easier to convince people that a change is needed. When the crisis itself is generating fear and uncertainty within the organization, it is much easier to get people on board with change.

If you've been an effective CEO, Charlie, you are implementing change before a crisis occurs. The change that your organization is about to go through is proactive and driven by a strategic vision that has identified the need to change due to all of those strategic analyses that we discussed earlier. The organization is making the needed change to be ahead of the predicted crisis or threat to the business that is looming in the future, or it is taking advantage of an opportunity to grow the business and its profitability.

> *The big challenge is that when change is proactive, the company today may be doing just fine, making money, and growing. What's the problem? Why do we need to change?*

61

Now is one of those times, Charlie, that, as an effective CEO, you need to clearly demonstrate your commitment to this change and show your organization why they pay you the big bucks. Now it's all about how you will educate your organization on why this change is needed and how you plan on communicating this need for change to your team.

Let's discuss a real-world example of this using your regional supermarket chain, Charlie.

A STORY

Charlie's company primarily competes head-on with a number of other supermarkets, including the large national chains and local independent grocers. The supermarket industry is highly competitive with very slim profit margins. The competitive landscape for supermarkets is highly complex and fragmented. Supermarkets compete with national drug store chains that now sell food, the "dollar store" formats that sell food, and even restaurants that have both dine-in and home-delivery options.

During their latest strategic planning initiative, the supermarket industry analysts from the consulting firm that Charlie hired identified a real and growing threat to their future operations. The large online retailer (named after a long river in Brazil) that had such a devastating impact on other retail formats (e.g. books, electronics) had recently set their sights on the supermarket industry as a major potential growth area for their company. This online retailer had been evaluating a number of brick-and-mortar supermarket chains to acquire so they could learn the business and eventually disrupt this multi-trillion-dollar industry with their online shopping capa-

(continued)

A STORY

bilities and business model. The consulting firm advised Charlie's company that they had about three to five years to prepare for this threat to their business.

The strategic initiative that was identified to address this impending threat was going to be a very large, very complex, and very expensive project. This project was going to involve adding several new components to the company's existing business model, implementing new technologies to support online shopping with in-store pick-up and home delivery options, a new organization to support this component of the business model, and integrating all of these changes into their current systems and database management environments. A true "omni-channel" initiative. This was estimated to be a three-year to four-year project with a capital price tag of $250 million. Piece of cake!

In the final strategic planning meeting and presentation, Charlie had a bead of sweat on her forehead as the consulting team discussed this omni-channel initiative. You see, Charlie knew that the company was currently doing very well. It was opening new stores, growing profits, and successfully competing for market share. She also knew that this initiative needed to be done, and it needed to start soon. Very few people in her organization would know of—or understand—this impending threat three to five years over the horizon. Successfully completing past change initiatives were difficult enough even when there was clear-and-present-danger in their company's environment. This was going to be a tough sell.

Charlie knew that it was time to convince her organization that the "oil platform was on fire!"

The best analogy that I ever used with clients faced with this challenge is the "Burning Oil Platform." The analogy: What does it take to make a person, or people, within the organization jump off a seemingly good and operational oil platform? Simple, they need to be convinced that the oil platform is *on fire* and if they don't jump, well, the consequences of what will happen in the not-too-distant-future are much worse than those shark-infested and cold waters down there! In my opinion, this is one of the more difficult aspects of proactive organizational change. Remember, it's all about people, and these people need to be convinced that the potential "pain and suffering" that change brings is needed and is needed now!

I have seen the full range of actions by organizations over the years, and unfortunately, in too many companies—and yes, with too many of my clients—the executives approached this challenge by plowing forward with the change, or more commonly referred to as the "I'm going to shove this change down your throat, and you're going to like it, or else."

Don't take that approach, Charlie! *Have I mentioned the 50-percent failure rate of organizational change initiatives?*

Your job, Charlie, is to demonstrate good leadership and clearly convince your organization that, yeah, things are going fine today. We're making money and everybody may be happy, but change in our industry, business, and competitive environment is coming, and *if we don't change now, where we are headed as an organization will be much worse than implementing this change into our business.* If you don't convince your organization that the oil platform is on fire, you will most likely meet with resistance from every level of the organization as you attempt to implement this change.

How do you do this, Charlie? I'll be honest, it ain't easy!

As with most aspects of successful organizational change, it should start with any effective strategic planning process. If the strategic plan has been done the right way, there are key people in the organization at multiple levels who have helped identify the growing threat to the business and have been part of the development of the strategies and needed changes to address this future threat. These key participants in the strategic plan are now your ambassadors and educators of this needed change. This makes your job a lot easier and your probability of success a lot higher.

This education process may require sharing information about your company, your industry, and your future strategies, which may not be comfortable to share. But I don't know any other way. Sure, as CEO, you are always sensitive to information about your company getting into the hands of a competitor. But let's discuss the worst-case scenario: Your competitor(s) finds out about this brilliant change that you are about to implement within your organization. They implement the change before your organization does, and they kick your butt! If that's the case, Charlie, shame on you for not implementing this change faster and giving your company the competitive advantage.

Educating an organization, or division, or department is easier said than done, and it will certainly depend on the size and culture of the organization, its complexity, and its geographic dispersion.

I don't know your company like you do, Charlie. Is the most effective way to communicate and educate your organization a top-down process that begins by educating the executive management levels of the organization? It is easier sharing information with these levels of the organization. If this top level of the organization is not convinced, well, good luck implementing anything! If you are successfully educating people at the executive management levels and are still getting resistance from certain people at these levels, it's time to get the right people "on the bus" before moving forward.

Is your organization small enough to get the whole team

together to discuss your strategic findings and the need for change? Will this change only impact certain departments or divisions? How will that impact the communication and education?

As I mentioned earlier in this book, nobody understands your organization like you, Charlie. Get your executive team together to discuss the best way to begin this communication and education and then *do it*! It may be hard, you may not be 100-percent successful, but you need to try and try hard. It will pay big dividends in the future.

Fig. 6.1 Picture of Burning Oil Platform

▲ *How do you get a person to jump off an oil platform? You need to convince them it's on fire! This is a great analogy for a CEO who needs to convince his/her team that they need to implement organizational change, even though things may be going well for the company today. "We're ready to jump, Charlie!"*

7 Let's Wash That Rental Car

I've rented so many cars in my life. I was such a good customer that I was in the "platinum" category with several car rental companies and was upgraded to the fancy schmancy class of car all the time. You know, the Lincoln Continentals, Cadillacs, and other "grandpa" cars. Looking back, do you know how many times I actually washed my rental car? You guessed right, none! Have you ever washed your rental car? Most likely not. And why not? Because you don't own it!

One of the most common problems with organizational change is very similar to the reason you don't wash a rental car. Really! People, departments, and organizations don't care about things they don't own. Successful organizational change is all about people taking ownership and buying into the change.

Here is a typical scenario that you will see—and I have seen—in many organizations embarking on a change initiative. It goes like this:

✓ A well-intentioned CEO recognizes the need to update the organization's strategic plan, so she hires a well-known consulting firm to help her develop the plan.

✓ The consultants are really smart and work really hard, and the strategic plan is completed with some—but minimal—employee involvement, and it's presented to the CEO. After some "cussing and discussing" between the CEO and her consulting team, the strategic plan is finalized.

✓ The CEO calls a meeting to present the plan to her team.

✓ She brings in copies of the plan in a three-ring binder. She takes one of the binders, holds it up, and says, "Here is our new strategic plan folks, and it's a great plan. It's genius."

✓ Now the people in her audience—you know, her team— are sitting out there thinking to themselves, "That may be your plan, Charlie, but it ain't ours."

✓ Hmm ... how do you think the implementation of that plan will go?

To that CEO's team, the new strategic plan is just like the rental car. They don't own it, and they're not going to wash it!

For your team to take *ownership* in the strategic plan, they needed to have *participated* in the strategic planning process. For your team to take *ownership* in the plan's goals and objectives, they needed to have *participated* in the development of the goals and objectives. Your team needs to believe it's *their* plan, and *their* goals and objectives. It makes perfect sense, right?

Unlike getting your team to jump off the oil platform, which is very hard, having them participate in the process and take ownership in the process is really not that hard or complex. You just have to *do it*, Charlie.

So, let's talk about how to do it.

It starts with the strategic planning process. Now, I certainly understand that organizations have different strategic planning processes, analyses, complexities, planning documents, etc. But remember, if you're doing your job right, the change that you are about to embark on is driven by the strategic plan. It's in the plan, right, Charlie?

Unlike the scenario described above, your team needs to be an integral part of the strategic planning process for it to be *their* plan. Obviously, you can't have your entire team on the strategic planning process, somebody has to operate the company. So, what do you do?

Here is one of the many important times to exhibit executive commitment. Smell the bacon, Charlie!

Whether it's putting together a team for a strategic planning project, or any project, or a change initiative that is being implemented as part of your overall organization's strategy, you'll want your best people on the project. If the project is important for your organization's success, it's important to have the best team working on it.

What do I mean by "best people"? Sometimes it's not that obvious.

The Top Ten key characteristics of a "best person" to put on a project include (not in any order of importance because they are all important):

- ✓ Respected by their peers: The key words here are "by their peers," not necessarily respected by management. If this person is respected by their peers for the right reasons, then it will be much easier for their peers to feel they are participating in this project through this person. This important topic is discussed later in this chapter.

- ✓ A "Rising Star": This is the person who the organization feels—at both the management and employee levels—has a bright and successful future in the organization and will continue to rise through the ranks.

- ✓ Smart: Well, you really don't want stupid people on your project team. This person will need to be smart and a good problem solver.

✓ Open minded, and a person who will embrace change: This characteristic may be a bit harder to pinpoint, but this person needs to have an attitude that embraces change. You may need to do some digging, interviewing, or reviewing performance evaluations to get this right.

✓ Good communicator: This person will be expected to communicate the status of the project back into the organization they came from. This requires good written and verbal communications.

✓ Good work ethic: Projects are demanding. Long hours may be required, and they will always be working under some type of deadline. I've never been on a project where long hours and deadlines weren't present. You need this person to be ready for this demanding work environment.

✓ Has expertise in the area, department, and function of the business being addressed (i.e. subject matter experts): One of the reasons you will pick this person is because they will help the team and the organization make good decisions. Functional expertise is important.

✓ The right level of technical skills: More often than not, change initiatives and projects involve some type of new technology. Depending on the role you want this person to play on the team, their level of technical skills needs to support this role. They may not need to be a technical "geek," but they will need to feel comfortable embracing new technologies.

✓ The right attitude: This is a very broad characteristic and includes several components:

  - Do they have the right level of maturity to work in

a demanding team environment where everything may not go right? When problems occur, how will they deal with these?

- Not a "yes man or yes woman": You will need this person to speak their mind in a team environment where other team members may be higher in the organization than they are. If they are afraid to disagree with one of their "superiors," then they may not add any value to the team.

- They need to be a good team player. Projects require good teamwork, and some people are better in this environment than others.

Do you have any people who fit this set of recommended characteristics, Charlie? I hope so. You will need to find these people in your organization. They may not be—and probably won't be—the obvious or initial choices like the VPs, assistant VPs, department heads, etc, and let's be honest, you may step on some people's toes by making these decisions.

I'm just going to say it and get it out there. It is certainly disappointing, but there have been many executives and managers whom I have met when working with my clients who have been perfect examples of the Peter Principle. This principle, which was coined by the famous management professor and author, Peter Drucker, says that a person "rises to the level of their incompetence."

Am I making myself clear? I am certainly not saying that all VPs, assistant VPs, department heads, etc. are incompetent, because most are not. What I am saying is that the Peter Principle is alive and well in many

○ *For the remainder of this chapter, let's again use the implementation of a new store labor-management system as our example of a change initiative and to discuss and learn how we can get the store operations organization to take ownership of this new system.*

organizations and should be a consideration when selecting key people to help your organization successfully implement change.

Back to the selection of the best people for your project. After discussions with your store operations management team and your human resources department, you've selected a rising-star store manager who has worked her way up through the ranks in store management and now runs one of the most successful and profitable stores in the chain. Let's call her Pam. She is highly respected by her fellow store managers, many of whom she has mentored over the past several years.

Next, you've selected a super-star district manager, who, like Pam, worked his way up through store management and was promoted to district manager several years ago. He now has twelve store managers reporting to him in one of the supermarket chain's most successful districts. Let's call him Bill. Bill is highly respected across store operations and is predicted to rise rapidly through the ranks and become the vice president of Operations in the not-so-distant future. Good choices, Charlie!

To illustrate where and how Pam and Bill fit into this project team, let's refer back to Figure 3.2: "The Players in Organizational Change" in Chapter 3. These two members of the project team will be representing the Operational Department, which will be directly impacted by this new store labor management system.

Both Pam and Bill fit the right characteristics described earlier and are excited about the opportunity to work on this highly important and impactful project for the company. Way to go, Charlie. You now have two excellent team members who will play a critical role of successfully implementing this change initiative.

Now, let's talk about what you do with these people once you find them. Well, do you smell the bacon, Charlie? Once

Fig. 7.1 Pam and Bill As Key Players

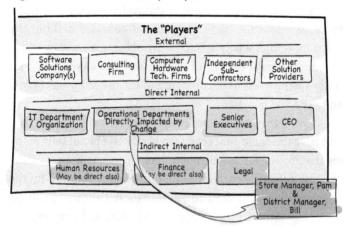

▲ *In Chapter 3, we discussed the players in an organizational change initiative. This diagram illustrates that two key employees, Pam and Bill, were pulled out of their full-time jobs and assigned to this project representing the Store Operations Department. They will be two key members of this project team that will be comprised of various internal and external resources.*

you've discussed this opportunity with Pam and Bill, and both of them agree that it's the right fit and career move for them, you *pull them both out of their current jobs and assign them to the project team full time.* Yes, you heard me right. Pam and Bill's jobs are now to help you successfully implement this change into the organization. And yes, Charlie, this takes executive commitment.

Obviously, these people joining your project team had full-time jobs, so they will need to be backfilled during the project. Depending on the estimated length of the project, this can be a temporary or permanent job alignment, but you can figure this out, Charlie. You have to keep the plane flying. (See Chapter 11.)

Also, depending on the size and geographic dispersion of the company, Pam and Bill may need to be re-located to the corporate office during the project timeframe. This is a big commitment for these people. To consider making this move more palatable for them, you should consider making the move more financially attractive by offering a raise in salary and/or a bonus at the end of the project. This would be a relatively small investment compared to the overall project costs and expected benefits.

Now, Pam and Bill are people too. Be assured that they will have the same concerns as anybody else about how being on the project for months—or even years—will affect their careers, future promotions, or other opportunities in the company. You will need to address these concerns right up front, but these are easy concerns to address. In my experience, the people who work on these projects become such valuable assets to the company that they typically rise very quickly through the organization. These people will not only have knowledge and experience in the system or technology implemented in their particular areas, but they will also have a great perspective of the entire business and its strategies and directions. Again, Pam and Bill will become very valuable assets to you and your organization, so make sure you tell them this. You obviously can't make promises at the front-end of any project, but, if they perform well, their career trajectories will be very positive. At a minimum, you need to guarantee that after the project, their old job will still be there for them, and their time on this project will be included in their "years of experience" when considering future promotions, raises, etc.

Another very important thing you must address with these team members, Charlie, is your need for both of them *not* to be a "yes man" or "yes woman." Make sure they understand that they were selected to work on this project because of their experience, intelligence, work ethic, and the fact that they are respected by their peers and by members of management. Tell them that on this project they will be working with people within the organization at multiple levels, including members of management higher than they are in the organization. They will also be working with members of the consulting firm that you plan on hiring to assist with the project. They need to clearly understand that you expect them to speak their minds and feel comfortable disagreeing with superiors or consultants, as long as these disagreements are intended to make the project and organization more successful. Honestly, Charlie, this is really hard for many people to do, especially ones who work in organizations with clearly defined hierarchies. These team members need to know that they have your support and that their jobs will not be in jeopardy if they disagree with their superiors or the consultants, as long as these are all handled professionally and not personally.

Finally, let's discuss the important topic of who Pam and Bill will report to during this project. Remember, this project may go for months, and perhaps years. I'll be honest, reporting relationships on project teams can be a bit squishy. During the project timeframe, they certainly need to be reporting to the project manager, if one of them is not assigned as project manager. They would also have a dotted line reporting relationship to the key executive responsible for this project, or to the steering committee that is overseeing this project. But remember, these key employees will need performance evaluations, raises, bonuses, etc., like all other employees. Someone who is responsible for this project needs to make sure these get done. In the consulting firm world, this type of reporting relationship is part of the culture, and consultants get used to it. But taking a person out of their job who has been in an organization with clear reporting relationships and career paths may feel very uncomfortable in this squishy project environment. Be conscious of this, make sure your human resources group is conscious of this, and manage it responsibly.

Now you have the right people from your operations organization to join the team of players illustrated above who will comprise you project team for this change initiative.

Let's briefly revisit the concept of this chapter: washing the rental car.

Remember, nobody washes a rental car because they don't own it. Likewise, people in organizations resist change when they have no ownership in that change. People are much more likely to take ownership in new ideas, new systems, new processes, or any new change when they have *participated* in the development of those ideas. It's human nature. Now we all know that we can't put everyone in the organization on the project team so they can participate in the process because somebody has to operate and run the stores!

Pam and Bill will certainly be *participating* in the process and will most certainly take *ownership* of the new change initiative, but how will the rest of the organization take ownership? Good question.

The concept is that other employees in the organization who work in the same areas in which Pam and Bill were pulled will feel they are participating *through Pam and Bill*. These employees will then feel comfortable and believe that Pam and Bill will be looking out for them.

For example, if I'm another store manager, and I see Pam and Bill being put on this project, and if I respect them and know that they understand the challenges and issues faced by the stores, then I will feel confident that they will be looking out for the stores in their roles on this project team. Furthermore, I will believe that they will not let the IT Department shove this new system down our throats. Therefore, I can feel that I am participating in this project *through Pam and Bill* with the overall objective of all the store managers feeling they are participating on the project through Pam and Bill. Finally, if the store managers feel they are participating, and they see

Pam and Bill taking ownership in this new system, well, the store managers across the chain can feel better about taking ownership in this new system. That's the concept. Remember, since we can't put everybody on the project team, having your organization feel they are participating in the project and taking ownership in the new system through the right team members is about as good as we can get, Charlie.

But as you would guess, Charlie, this concept of participation and ownership of the new system across the store operations organization doesn't just happen. It takes a concerted and proactive effort on your part, Pam and Bill's part, and on the whole project team's part. This concerted and proactive effort involves two critical activities throughout the project: communication and education.

In the previous chapter, Charlie, you did a great job of convincing your organization that the oil platform is on fire, and that, as hard as it may be, implementing the needed change in the organization is much better than not moving forward. Long experience in this industry of helping companies make the leap off the oil platform has taught me that as you move forward with the change, the organization will need to be, well, reminded that making this change is the best way forward.

Two of the key roles that Pam and Bill will play on this project will be communicating back into their organization the status of the project, the major decisions being made on the new system, and the completion of major milestones as they are reached. In addition, during this communication process, Pam and Bill should continue to educate their organization as to why this project is so important for the business and what it will mean to the organization.

Depending on the size of their organization and the geographic dispersion of people in it, there will be some factors that will have to be considered to determine what method or platform this communication will take. This can range from group meetings in smaller organizations, to newsletters, project blog sites, emails, or other types of internal communication protocols.

You can figure out the best method for your organization, Charlie. But the key is to communicate to the organization—or those departments that are directly impacted by this change—on a regular basis. This communication will include, at a minimum, the status and progress of the project, major milestones accomplished, and what will be happening on the project over the next weeks or months. Pam and Bill will play a key role in formulating this communication. They speak the same language as the stores. It won't be some IT guy or consultant speaking in "gobbledygook" that the store employees might not understand. Pam and Bill are one of them and should have direct and open communications with store operations. And yes, Charlie, you have to communicate the good, the bad, and the ugly. Remember, every organization has a very effective "grapevine." If you only communicate the good news, the bad news will get out there anyway, and you run the risk of losing credibility in the eyes of the organization.

* * *

In this chapter, we've been using a store labor management project as our example, and we have pulled out two store operations employees (Pam and Bill) to work full time on this project. But let's be realistic about the number of people who will need to be pulled out of the business for your project, Charlie. As usual, the answer is "it depends."

Now, this is not a project management book, but in Chapter 3, we discussed the Change Model and the players involved in projects. Depending on the scope of the project, the size of the organization, and the complexity of the change initiative, this project team can be sizeable.

During the initial project approval, planning, and organization phase of this initiative, some type of work plan will be developed that includes the tasks to be completed, estimated time frames, skills needed, etc. So, based on this work plan, the size of the project team, the skills needed on the project team, etc. will all be determined. I'm trying not to be wishy-washy here, but the number of people to pull out of your organization will depend on this work plan, the role of the consultants (if any), the role of other vendors, the number of your IT people on the project, etc. I have worked on very large projects in very large organizations, where five to six operational employees at different levels were pulled out of their jobs and assigned to the project full time. So, if it helps, five to six operational people were the most I've ever seen assigned full time to a project. But again, Charlie, it all depends on your situation. Was that wishy-washy?

So, Charlie, let's get the bucket and soap and wash that rental car!

8 Ready ... Aim ... FIRE!

A re you a good decision maker, Charlie? This chapter is all about "pulling the trigger," or commonly known as: making a decision.

In Chapter 4, we discussed the "culture for change." One of the most important cultural aspects for successful organizational change is how decisions are made, how comfortable people are making decisions, and how the organization treats people when they have made good—or bad—decisions. Nothing much happens in an organization without decisions being made, so let's talk about this important aspect of successful organizational change.

The title of this chapter (Ready ... Aim ... Fire!) implies the decision-making process.

Let's first talk about the "Aim," or the analysis. What is the right amount of analysis that is needed before a decision is made? Good question. There is certainly a lot of literature on this topic, but I'll try to keep this simple. For example, if your project team is deciding on where to go for lunch, well, there's probably not a lot of analysis needed. If your team is working on a project to evaluate and select a new software solution from a group of vendors

Ready: *the organization, or project team, is at the point where a decision is needed;* **Aim**: *the right amount of analysis is done in order to make the best decision;* **Fire**: *the decision is made and the project moves forward. Simple, right?*

and deciding on which vendors' software they will recommend—which may cost gobs of money to license and install and will impact the business for many years to come—well, probably more analysis will be needed than the lunch decision. But how much?

I look at the "Aim" as a spectrum of analysis. On one end of this spectrum is the "Ready, Fire, Aim" scenario where decisions are made too quickly without enough analysis. On the other end is the "Ready; Aim, Aim, Aim, Aim" where you've reached "analysis paralysis." You're perhaps looking for the perfect decision, but a decision is perhaps never made, or at least significantly delayed.

Let's use a picture to illustrate this Aim spectrum. Figure 8.1 (below) shows that the more analysis that is done for a

Fig. 8.1 Diagram on Decision-Making Analysis

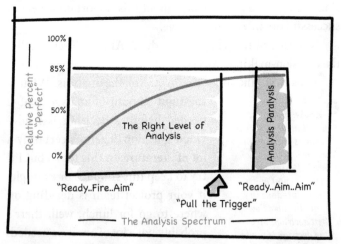

▲ *This diagram graphically illustrates the balance between performing analysis for an important decision, and the act of making the decision, or "pulling the trigger." Perfect decisions are rarely made, so it's important to pull the trigger after the right amount of analysis, but before you reach the point of diminishing returns from that analysis. It is never a good place to be in the "analysis paralysis" zone. Don't let that happen, Charlie!*

decision, the closer that decision approached "perfect," but then the analysis reaches a point of diminishing returns, and you enter the dreaded "analysis paralysis" zone.

At some point during the analysis, a decision needs to be made.

Over the years, I have had the discussion with clients on many occasions that essentially goes like this: "You will never make a perfect decision. It's better to make a somewhat-flawed decision (e.g. 85 percent of perfect), and successfully implement that decision, than to keep waiting for the perfect decision." Genius!

Here is an example of this situation:

I spent a lot of my consulting career helping clients select software packages for various parts of their businesses. The typical approach was to perform a "requirements definition" for both business functions and technology requirements. Then a detailed Request for Proposal (RFP) was generated and sent to a list of leading software vendors, who would respond in writing to the RFP with complete honesty, of course. The vendors' responses would be tabulated and the top three or four-ish would be asked to give presentations on their software. Based on all this analysis, the team would make a recommendation to the steering committee, and the process would move forward with contract negotiations, perhaps a pilot implementation, and then the general implementation of the software into the business. Piece of cake!

Over the years, I have helped many clients through this type of software selection with a very rigorous RFP process. Unfortunately, I've had more than one client that went through the process and, well, let's just say they had trouble "pulling the trigger." In most of these cases, there were two software solutions that were very, very close to one another in how well they met the client's requirements, so the recommendation by the team (or the steering committee) was to perform a pilot implementation for both software packages! What??? Time to coach my client.

Let's think this through. The company is performing this selection process because they have identified business benefits and improvements from implementing new software, functionality, and processes. Now we're going to complete a three-, six-, or nine-month (or longer) pilot on *two* systems in order to make the best decision for the future software? Okay, let's think ahead three, six, or nine months, and now we've completed the two pilots. Are we any closer to a decision? The reality is that the success of the pilots will be more to do with *how* the pilot was organized and implemented, rather than the specific software package. In addition, there will certainly be pros and cons that the pilot identifies for each software package, and most software companies will charge you for this pilot, so there will be added costs. Are we any closer to a decision, or have we just delayed the benefits to the business for three, six, or nine months?

In all of these client situations, I have tried to coach my client by advising them that if these two software packages are both that close to their requirements, then put the two vendors' names on the wall, throw a dart, and pick the one where the dart lands! Wow, that's great consulting! But the reality is that if these two software packages are that close to your requirements, then the success of this project—and ultimately the business receiving the expected benefits—is all about *successful implementation*. So, let's pick one and get the implementation right!

The lesson here is that there is no magic formula or Ouija board to indicate when the right amount of analysis has been completed and it's time to pull the trigger. I think what is important is that the team or person making the decision or the recommendation is conscious of this spectrum of analysis and continues the analysis until a point of diminishing returns is recognized. The team needs to discuss this at the front-end of the analysis and decision-making process and have some type of metric or process in place to understand when that point is reached. Remember, as I discussed in my "two-pilot" client story, the longer you delay your decision, the longer it will take for your organization to achieve the benefits from this change initiative.

Now let's talk about the "FIRE!" When a decision is made, it's important to remember the "ownership" issue from the previous chapter. If you want your team and organization to take ownership in the decision being made, they need to be part of that process.

Another important consideration that is fairly common is when a team that is tasked to make a recommendation cannot reach consensus on that recommendation. Remember, these are people who bring their own experience, prejudices, feelings, and emotions into the decision-making process and, well, sometimes people don't all agree. The last thing that the project needs is to move into the *analysis paralysis phase* where the team becomes incapable of making a decision. It's time for you, Charlie (or the right executive), to step in, evaluate the decision-making process to this point, evaluate the risks, pros, and cons, and then pull the trigger!

Remember, there are no perfect decisions. The important thing now is to implement this decision as successfully as possible. If your team is in the "analysis paralysis" zone, and they understand that they are having trouble coming to consensus, I believe they will respect an executive to step in and make the call. I think your team would expect you—or one of your executives—to do their job and pull the trigger.

And Charlie, I know that you know there are inherent problems in the decision-making process because remember, we are dealing with people. This is not a book on decision making, but let's briefly discuss some of these problems and weaknesses so your team can be aware of them, with the goal of not becoming an issue for your organization.

- ✓ **Voting:** This is when the group gives up on reaching a consensus and just votes for the decision. Not that voting is good or bad, but make sure the group has done sufficient analysis and worked hard on consensus before reaching the "let's vote" step.

- ✓ **CYA:** The old saying was "Nobody ever got fired for picking IBM." Ah yes, remember those days? CYA, also known as "cover your ass," is when a decision is made because it's the safe one to make, not necessarily the best one. This phenomenon is often found in organizations with a corporate culture that penalizes people or teams for making the wrong—or risky—decision.

- ✓ **Bounded rationality:** This is an important one to remember. Bounded rationality is the "you only know what you know" syndrome. I've seen this happen many times when companies are identifying the various alternatives to analyze for a decision, and they are not aware of all of the options available because they only know what they know. So, Charlie, make sure the team digs enough to discover all of the options available for an upcoming decision. Another good approach here is to hire a consulting firm to help with identifying the options. Third party consulting firms are typically aware of what is available in the marketplace, or at least they should be aware.

- ✓ **Politics:** Simply stated, politics is all about "me." When an executive, or project manager, or even a team makes a "political decision," that decision is not necessarily for the benefit of the organization, but rather for the benefit of the person making the decision. Politics are present in every organization with varying degrees of "dis-functionality." Be aware of the political environment in which decisions are being made, Charlie. Remember, you can tell when a bad decision or recommendation is being made due to politics because all of a sudden, the room stinks!

✓ **Satisficing:** This situation occurs when the team makes a decision for the first alternative that meets most of the requirements, rather than evaluating all of the alternatives. This situation occurs when the decision maker gets lazy and really doesn't care about the quality of the outcome. Make sure your team is performing the right level of analysis.

✓ **Escalation of commitment:** This phenomenon occurs *after* a bad decision is made, but the team is so committed to their decision that they are incapable of pulling the plug and admitting it was the wrong decision. For example, the team picked a new and risky technology platform that they recently discovered was not ready for prime time, and now they all know it was potentially a bad decision, but they are so committed to that decision that the discussion goes like this: "We still have confidence in this vendor and we can still make this work."

The team keeps digging their hole deeper, and nobody has the courage to pull the plug because they will be admitting failure. Wiser heads realize that it is time to pull the plug and go back to the drawing board.

This list is certainly not exhaustive, but Charlie, make sure you and your team are aware of these potential traps as you start this decision-making process.

So, are you ready, Charlie? Ready ... Aim ... FIRE!

9 Keep Your Eyes on the Prize

Charlie, this chapter is about "scope management." Remember in Chapter 5 (Eggs & Bacon) where we discussed that the number one reason for organizational change failure is executive commitment? Well, the number two reason in my experience is poor scope management.

What is *scope?* In the simplest term, scope is what you need to do to achieve your anticipated benefit to the business. No more, and no less! The classic example to explain scope management is like building a house. Let's say that my wife and I are retiring, and we are going to build a home in a beautiful community in the Southwest to begin our retirement. The architects draw up the detailed architectural plans for building the house, then the designers help us pick the fixtures, tile, carpet, cabinets, etc., and they put that in the designer's plans. Then the landscape architects … okay … you get the picture. Now we have the plans to build our new house, and those plans are the *scope* of our building process. The builder commits to get the house done in twelve months for an estimated budget of $1 million. My wife and I can now begin to plan our wonderful retirement.

When the construction begins, we go to the builder and say, "We would like to add a casita (fourth bedroom) to the house." (i.e. scope expansion, or scope creep). One month later we go to the builder and say, "We would like to add a swimming pool." (i.e. scope expansion). Two months later, we go to the builder and say, "We would like to add a work shed with a fourth garage in the yard." (i.e. scope expansion). You get the picture. Now our twelve-month project has expanded to become a twenty-four-month project, and our budget has now increased by 30 percent. Our poor management of scope has delayed our retirement plans and now we can barely afford the house!

Yikes!!! That, Charlie, is scope management, or in this case, scope mismanagement. Make sense?

* * *

Now, let's go back to your business and talk about scope management for the store labor management project.

Through your strategic plan, you have identified the need for a new store labor management system and processes in order to improve store productivity and customer service. Your team—and consulting firm—have planned the project, estimated the capital requirements, developed a schedule for completion, and the related return-on-investment (ROI) for the change initiative. You have now planned a two-year project that will cost $5.3 million to complete, with an estimated ROI of 22 percent. All of those plans, cost estimates, and completion schedules are now your *scope* for this project. When this project is complete and your business is using this new software, technologies, and processes, the stores will be operating more efficiently. Your return-on-investment of 22 percent is now your "prize to keep your eyes on." Make sense? Great!

Then, during a steering committee meeting three months into the project, your IT executive presents her recommendation to implement the software vendor's new cloud-based version of the software. This new version is just now in the testing phase at the vendor, but it should be ready for deployment to customers in two months. In addition, this new cloud-based version will be running on a new database that the IT Department has been wanting to implement for a couple of years. As part of her presentation, your IT executive says, "This project presents a great opportunity for us to add these new features and technologies that our business has wanted for some time." She later adds the analogy of while the patient is on the operating table, let's do some more work to improve the patient. After some "cussing and discussing" the steering committee decides to approve your IT executive's recommendation.

Do you feel a weird tingling sensation down your spine, Charlie?

Three months later, in the next steering committee meeting, your HR executive proposes that while we are implementing a new store labor management system, it's the perfect opportunity to implement the vendor's new HR and payroll system that the business has needed for a few years. Your IT executive agrees with this recommendation, and again, after much debate, the steering committee approves expanding the project to include the vendor's new HR and payroll system as a joint project. Has that tingling down your spine returned, Charlie?

So now, Charlie, your two-year project with a 22-percent ROI, which will improve your store productivity and customer service, has now morphed into a four- to five-year project. The ROI has become so "mumboed jumboed" (technical term) that nobody understands what the original scope was. Everybody has taken their eyes off the prize. The dreaded "scope creep."

Finally, at a steering committee meeting three years down the road, the project has become too complicated, over budget, and delayed again, with no end in sight. Honestly, Charlie, I've seen this happen firsthand. Can anybody smell an utterly failed project? And yes, Charlie, one of the symptoms of scope creep is a weird tingling sensation down your spine during steering committee meetings.

Let's discuss the right way to manage this scope creep and keep your projects from heading down this slippery slope to failure. Just remember to keep your eyes on the prize.

During the now infamous steering committee meetings where the IT and HR executives are presenting their recommendations for scope expansion, the discussion that the steering committee needs to have goes something like this:

✓ That is a very interesting proposal, IT executive/HR executive, but we have identified a clear strategic objective to improve our store productivity and customer service in order to be more competitive in our industry. We have scoped that project with a two-year time horizon, a $5.2 million capital budget, and an anticipated ROI of 22 percent over five years.

✓ How will your proposed scope expansion (i.e. new database and cloud-based software version, or the new HR and payroll system) affect the time horizon, the capital expense, and more importantly, the ROI?

✓ How will your proposed scope expansion put the overall project at risk due to added complexity, time, and costs?

✓ All of those add-on projects sound like initiatives that we need to do at some point in the future, but we are going to stick to our plan and initial scope. We need to get this store labor management system done successfully. Let's address these add-on projects as separate initiatives that we can plan, scope, cost out, and manage without jeopardizing our store labor management system.

✓ Way to go, Charlie! You just kept your eyes on the prize.

I think it's appropriate in this chapter to discuss a potential "pink flag" that you need to be aware of if you are using a consulting firm to assist with your project. For your information, the next book in this series is called: *Don't Sign That Contract, Charlie: A CEO's Guide to Hiring and Managing Consultants,* which will go into much more detail on this issue, but consulting firms are always under pressure to increase revenues. An old saying in the consulting industry is: "The easiest engagement to sell is to a current client."

It is not uncommon—in fact, I would say it's more common than not—that your consulting firm will approach you with recommended scope increases or new add-on projects. In all fairness to consulting firms, these may be good ideas for your business. A common discussion point by consulting firms will be: "While we have the consulting team here, let's keep them together and working on these new initiatives." (Or something like that.) And sometimes that can make sense.

But the response is the same as the bullet points above. Keep your eyes on the prize, Charlie.

10 Pace: You Want It Done When?

Every organization has its own pace at which it can imple-ment change. Too fast and the project may fail. Too slow and you delay the benefits, or the project never gets done.

I'll be honest, there is no magic formula to determine the right pace for any project. But there are certainly aspects of your organization—and things to consider and discuss—when you determine the right pace. Those include:

✓ size of the organization that is being impacted by the project

✓ geographic dispersion of the organization

✓ number of locations to convert

✓ number of people to convert

✓ organization's culture for change

✓ complexity of the change

Since every organization is different, the *pace* of the project needs to be an important discussion topic during the project-planning phase.

Also, there are different pace considerations during the various phases of a project. Let's discuss some considerations using our store labor management example again:

✓ During the "system preparation" phase, where the

project team is working on tasks such as software configuration, data conversions, and any custom programming or development, the pace will be determined by things like:

- number of tasks to complete

- complexity of the tasks

- how many team members are available to complete these tasks

- whether these resources have the right expertise for the tasks

- what the task dependencies are (i.e. We can't start Task Five until Task Four is complete.)

✓ During any pilot, rollout, or conversion phase where you are now involving stores, departments, and employees that are "out in the business" and not part of your project team, some of the big issues to discuss when determining pace include:

- How different is this new system, set of processes and procedures, etc. from their current environment? For example, if the stores are going from a manual scheduling system (e.g. using Microsoft Excel) to a complex computerized system, that will certainly take longer for training compared to going from one computerized system to another computerized system.

- What training approach will you use? Will training be performed in a classroom setting? Will it be done online? Will a team of trainers need to go on site to train new users?

- How many locations will need to be piloted and converted? How much hand holding will need to be done by your project team during this phase? How geographically dispersed are these locations?

Again, there is no magic formula for the right pace. But it is important to consciously discuss the pace with your team and consultants during the planning phase of the project. In addition, have some contingencies in place in case the assumptions made on pace turn out to be, well, aggressive.

Finally, another "pink flag" when using consulting firms: For some reason, consultants are famous for setting unrealistic deadlines for completing tasks or project phases. Not to say that you shouldn't push your project team to get things done expeditiously, but make sure there is a good driving (and reasonable) justification for aggressive deadlines.

So, Charlie, what is the right pace for your organizational change initiative?

11 Keep the Plane Flying

A s we begin this chapter, Charlie, let's take a break and review what you've accomplished.

- ✓ You can smell the bacon and have committed yourself and other executives.

- ✓ You've convinced your organization that the oil plat-form is on fire and that they should all jump!

- ✓ You've taken the right steps to ensure that the organiza-tion will take ownership in the new change, so they can go and wash the rental car.

- ✓ You and your organization are making good decisions, after the right amount of analysis!

- ✓ You are managing your scope properly and keeping the organization's eyes on the prize.

- ✓ The organization has set an aggressive, but comfortable, pace for the organizational change.

Great job, Charlie! Now we need to keep the plane flying!

A great analogy that I have used with clients to discuss an important aspect of major organizational change is that organizational change is like switching out the engines on a 747 at 37,000 feet! What does this mean? Two very important things to remember:

1. Organizational change is hard to do successfully, just like switching out the engines on a plane at 37,000 feet.

2. As the organization is going through this change, you still have to *keep the plane flying.* You still have to run your business, take care of customers, and stay competitive. You cannot take your eye off the ball because, as you know, your competitors won't give you any slack.

Keeping the plane flying takes a conscious effort. Organizational change often takes years, and during that timeframe, the business world and your competitors are moving forward. You have to have a *keep-the-plane-flying* (KTPF) strategy in place.

Let's talk about what that means, and what that looks like. And let's be clear about when this is important. If your organizational change (OC) strategies, plans, project, etc. are limited in scope and affecting a small part of the organization, it's much easier to focus on your day-to-day business, and a KTPF strategy is not that important.

If your OC plans and strategies are big and taking significant time and energy from your executives and other key members of your management team, then the KTPF strategy needs to be incorporated into your overall OC strategy and plan!

As the project team is reporting on progress/status/milestones/etc., the KTPF team is also reporting on business operations and performance.

The OC project team and the KTPF team cannot be operating in silos! They must be coordinated with senior executive commitment and focus in order to make the needed decisions and focus the needed resources to keep both efforts moving forward successfully.

Here is a great example of what happens when the plane begins to lose altitude during a significant OC effort.

A STORY

One of my very best clients was a major supermarket and drugstore company that had become one of the largest in their industry through acquisitions. The corporate office had been run as a "management model" for years, letting their various corporate acquisitions run as autonomous businesses. A new CEO came on board and made the strategic decision to turn the company into an "operating business model," where the company would take advantage of its size in driving efficiencies in purchasing, distribution, etc. This was the largest and most complex organizational change that I had ever experienced with a client. This involved taking six independent companies with their own systems and technologies, distribution centers, management teams, etc., and creating one operating company with common systems, processes, distribution networks, etc.

Wow! My consulting firm was hired to assist with one of many projects. The overall effort was named the Delta Project. (You know, delta, meaning change.) Top executives (operational and IT) were pulled out of the business to focus on the Delta Project. The Delta Project even had its own office building. Really!

The organization was so focused on the Delta Project that it took its eye off the ball in running its day-to-day business, and the plane started to lose altitude. Store performance began to erode, and as you know, Wall Street doesn't care that much about your Delta Project, so the company's stock price began to fall.

About three years into the Delta Project, the company was acquired by one of their big competitors, and the plane crashed.

(continued)

A STORY

The ugliness of the acquisition is for another story (and another book), but the point is: this great company did not keep the plane flying!

So, Charlie, keep your plane flying!

Fig. 11.1 Picture/Illo of Flying Plane

▲ *Organizational change is like switching the engines out on a 747 at 37,000 feet! The two important things to remember from this analogy are: 1) organizational change is hard; and 2) while you're switching out these engines at 37,000 feet, you need to keep the plane flying! You need to keep running your business effectively because your competitors will not give you any slack.*

12 Celebrate, but Not for Too Long

When projects end successfully, it's because a lot of hard work has been accomplished by a team of your employees, your consultants, your vendors, et al. I believe that it's important to celebrate the accomplishment—or even a major milestone—toward that final accomplishment.

Why celebrate? Like I said in Chapter 4: it's all about people. When celebrations occur, it demonstrates that you and the executive team understand and appreciate the level of work that was done and the sacrifices that may have been made. It's a very important message that you will be sending to your team and to the rest of your organization.

What does "celebrate" mean? Good question, and I think this depends on the organization, its culture, its size, and its geographic dispersion. Is it a party? Maybe. Is it a company-wide meeting where recognition is given? Maybe. Is it a bonus check for the team? Maybe. Perhaps it's all of the above. But it needs to be something that these key employees see as valuable, meaningful, and appropriate.

Does your company have a track record for celebrations, Charlie? This can really be a cultural thing. Some organizations celebrate too much, and others not enough. You certainly know your "culture for celebration," and you can certainly figure out what the right—and appropriate—level of celebration is for your organization. In my opinion, celebrations are important. Projects are hard, and celebrating successes are not only important for those key employees on the team, but it's important for the rest of the organization to see how these people are treated, so when you ask them to get involved in the next project, they will/should be much more willing and interested.

But don't forget, Charlie, when you celebrate, you're setting a precedent for future celebrations. If you have a pizza party for this project (Please, Charlie, don't be that kind of cheapskate!), then you've set the celebration bar pretty low for the next project. But, if you give out bonuses for this project, you've set the precedent for future project celebrations!

So, Charlie, pick the right level for your culture and organization and celebrate! But not for too long.

The final topic in my strategic planning class was about implementing the strategies that were developed during the planning process. For the wrap-up discussion on this important topic, I gave my students the Top Ten of implementations. They were all humorous (it was a long and hard semester), but true, and the last one was "It Never Ends." It's very true. In today's complex and competitive world, organizations don't finish a project and say: "Okay, now let's take a few years off and put the company in neutral." It just doesn't happen.

The party is over. Time to get back to work, Charlie!

13 Where's the Beef? Or, Is That an Ugly "ROI Gap" I See Growing?

I bet you're exhausted, Charlie! Think about what you've done. First, you read this book, and then you ordered copies for your entire project team, right? You've done all the right things to get your change initiative completed successfully, and rumor has it, the project was completed on time and on budget! The consultants are now gone, the project team is disbanded, and it's back to business as usual. Congratulations!

I really hate to be the one to tell you this, Charlie, but you're not quite done yet. Sorry.

After the celebration party, there is still one more phase of the project to complete: Measuring the ROI the organization is achieving from the implementation of this change. It's all about metrics. Or, to use a catchphrase from an old fast food restaurant commercial: *Where's the Beef?*

The major driving reason for this project was for the strategic benefits it was going to provide to the organization. Remember the ROI? This ROI was developed using assumptions of business improvements such as increased revenues, increased margins, improved labor efficiencies, inventory turnover, etc. Is anybody going to measure whether these assumptions are panning out? Where's the Beef?

In my thirty years of working with clients to implement change in their organizations, I can't give you a single example of a company that did this. In all fairness, most consulting contracts end and the consultants go away after the implementation party (or after they get fired for not being successful, but that's another book), and they don't have the exposure to see if this "Where's the Beef?" phase ever gets done. But if I were a betting man …

Now you may be saying: "Bob, why is this so important? We followed all of your advice, we got the project completed successfully, and the new system is now part of our business and culture. So, lighten up, Bob."

Not so fast, Charlie! If you are not consciously tracking and measuring those important metrics, how do you know that the system is being used to its full potential? How do you know that there isn't an ROI gap growing between *is achieving* and *should be achieving*, and thus leaving benefits on the table? You don't. So, measure it.

I certainly know that many—if not most—of these benefit areas (e.g. revenue, margins, inventory turnover, labor efficiencies, etc.) are all tracked as normal parts of your financial and operational reporting and analysis every week, month, quarter, etc. I also understand that there are many factors (internal and external to the company) that influence and impact these benefit areas, not just changes implemented from this project. The business world is a dynamic and moving target, and it's difficult to look back through the one, two, or three years it took to complete your project and do an apples-to-apples comparison. I get it!

However, that is no excuse for not understanding whether you are achieving the benefits in your business from this new change, and if not, what can you do differently, or better, to drive more improvements? How are the benefit areas stacking up to the assumptions made during the initial project ROI development?

Let's use our store labor management project as the example to discuss how these metrics can be tracked to ensure that your organization is not developing an ROI Gap. This "gap" concept is important, so let's use a simple diagram below to illustrate it.

Let's take a trip down memory lane, Charlie.

Remember three years ago when the project team was presenting the anticipated benefits and related ROI to the capital committee for this store labor management project? The benefits (albeit a simplified example) from implementing this comprehensive system and related processes included:

✓ The reduction of wasted labor in the stores due to improved labor requirement forecasts and weekly labor schedules.

Fig. 13.1 ROI Gap Chart

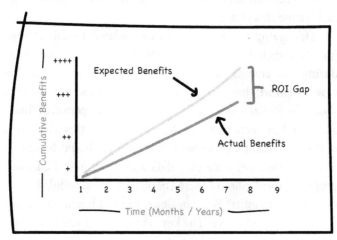

▲ *This graph illustrates the concept of a growing ROI gap. If your organization fails to evaluate the metrics from a major organizational change, you run the risk of achieving lower benefits to the business than were expected, perhaps without even being aware of these lost benefits. Do you have a growing ROI gap, Charlie?*

✓ Increase in sales due to improved customer service from having the right number of store associates in the store when customers are shopping.

✓ Based on the two business improvements above, the metric of sales/labor hour was projected to increase by 5 percent, resulting in labor cost reductions of $1.2 million per year.

We all know that metrics such as store revenue/sales, store labor hours and related costs, and customer counts are all tracked and reported on a regular basis, along with a bunch of other metrics, figures, and statistics, and we can't see the "ROI Gap Forest for the Trees." Is there an ROI gap? Is it growing? Do we even know?

Let's talk about this final "Where's The Beef?" phase of your change initiative. This phase should be planned for at the beginning of—or during—the project so everyone knows it's going to happen, and we know the metrics that will be revisited during this phase.

Depending on some key factors related to this change initiative, including: the area of the business being addressed during this change; the anticipated rate of change that this new system will have on this area of the business (e.g. benefits should be realized quickly versus over a longer period of time); additional projects that may be underway in this same area of the business; etc., follow-up checkpoints should be scheduled to collect any necessary data and develop an ROI analysis/assessment. Should these checkpoints be scheduled every three or six months? You can figure this out based on the key factors discussed above. The key is to get them scheduled and get them done.

Who should participate in these ROI analysis/assessment checkpoints? My recommendation is a sub-set of the same cast of characters who started and approved this change initiative. These will include you, Charlie; members of the capital committee; members of the project team; and yes, a set of the consultants you engaged to help you. (I realize you'll have to pay them, but it's worth it!)

Prior to the big checkpoint meeting, members of your project team should be collecting the needed data and preparing the reports, presentation, etc. that will be used for ROI analysis/assessment discussions. If the preliminary results of this data collection and analysis indicate some issues and concerns for a possible ROI gap, some additional digging for data may be required for the meeting. Let's use an example of our store labor management system for this additional digging:

- ✓ Preliminary analysis of our sales/labor hour metric has only increased 3 percent since the new system was implemented versus the anticipated 5-percent increase. What's going on?

- ✓ Are there other factors influencing this metric that we need to consider so we are looking at an apples-to-apples comparison? For example: Is there a new labor union contract in place affecting minimum hours? Have we made changes in our stores since the project was started that impact labor requirements, such as self-checkout lanes, cafes, or online shopping with store pick-up?

- ✓ How is the new system being used in the stores? Are the store managers using the new system correctly? Are computer-generated schedules being overridden by the managers? Should we survey the store managers on their assessments of the new system?

- ✓ Let's get this data organized and prepared for the check-point meeting with some preliminary assessments and recommendations.

* * *

Now, let's talk about this meeting, and let's remember Chapter 2 on "Culture for Change." If the data indicates that the anticipated ROI is being achieved, great; let's schedule the next meeting to continue our assessment. If the data indicates there is an ROI gap, and the benefit metrics are not being met, and this meeting turns into a finger-pointing and witch hunt session, well, you're wasting your time, and your project was probably a failure anyway.

This meeting is all about:

- ✓ What can we do to get better?

- ✓ What can we do to close this ROI gap?

- ✓ Have we configured the system properly?

- ✓ Do we need to have follow-up training?

- ✓ Have we communicated our expectations to each store effectively?

- ✓ Do we need to be collecting additional data?

Let's put some action plans in place to begin closing this ROI gap. Good meeting, Charlie!

Based on the results of this meeting, there may be a mini-project that needs to be planned and implemented to make the needed changes to close this ROI gap.

I know, Charlie, this ain't easy, and it never ends!

14 You're Right, It's Hard!

Let's wrap this book up!

Driving organizational change in any business is hard. Keeping your company competitive is hard. The business world is hard, but we know that.

As I stated at the beginning of this book, the implementation of change into a complex organization has a lousy track record of success. Even after all of the business books that have been written on this topic and the textbooks that business students study that address this topic, organizations keep failing at this fundamental part of the business world. Yes, it's hard. But failing to lead your organization through the changes needed to stay competitive is unacceptable.

I hope this book has helped you and your organization to successfully implement change.

ACKNOWLEDGMENTS

Since this is my first book, I want to thank and acknowledge not only the people who helped me with my rookie experience of becoming an author, but also those people who played an important role in my thirty-seven-year career as a consultant, entrepreneur, CEO, and college professor. After all, it was this amazing career that gave me all those experiences, all those stories, and all those successes and screw-ups that led me to become an author.

None of my success in either my professional or personal life would have been possible without my wife, Kathy, who has been my best friend for fifty-one years and my wife for forty-one years. We went to high school, college, and graduate school together. We raised an amazing son together. Kathy held our home and family together while I hopped on airplanes almost every week for thirty years. She trusted me when I told her I wanted to quit my six-figure-salary consulting job to start my own company. She trusted me when I told her that we had to take (more) money out of our savings to make payroll during the lean times that all small businesses face. Thank you, Kathy!

I also want to thank all of those consulting partners with whom I worked during the twenty years I spent with three large global consulting firms. I may not have respected all of them, but I certainly learned from all of them. Then, of course, there was the great team of professionals who worked with me in my company. We were always a small, boutique firm, but these men and women were some of the best and brightest in their areas of specialization within the U.S. retail industry. I had a great team.

After thirty years in the business world, I sold my company to a British firm, retired, and started my second career as a college professor. For seven years, I had both the opportunity and privilege to walk into the classroom with amazing young people, literally from all over the world, and teach them about business management, strategy, and entrepreneurship, as well as all of those stories and lessons I learned over a great thirty-year business career. The classroom can be a magical experience, and it was for me. It was the highlight of my career. I can't tell you how many times my students (or my "kids" as I called them) told me that I needed to record my lectures and put them on YouTube or write books about my knowledge and experiences in the business world. Well, kids, I did it! Thank you!

Writing a book is a challenging and interesting journey. I certainly want to thank those people who made this journey enjoyable and hopefully successful. These people include my colleagues and mentors: Michael Glauser, PhD, Melissa Koerner, PhD, Alysse Morton, PhD, and Bob Henson. Thank you for your advice and encouragement. I also want to thank three colleagues and friends with whom I worked in my professional career who gave me advice and stories as well as encouragement through this process. These great guys are Frank Eckstein, Charles (Chuck) Cagle, and Alan Williams. Thanks, gentlemen!

I also want to thank Layne Lundstrom. I worked with Layne while I owned and ran my company. Layne developed my company's website, our marketing materials, and all of our branding. When I started working on my book, I contacted Layne to help me develop my platform. He has done that and has also developed all of the illustrations in this book. He is one of the most talented and passionate people with whom I have worked in my career. Thanks, Layne.

Finally, I would like to thank my publisher, Lisa Akoury-

Ross, and my editors Robert Astle and Katie Barger. These three professionals have been instrumental in coaching me through this process. I could not have finished this book without them. Thank you, Lisa, Robert, and Katie.

ABOUT THE AUTHOR

Robert J. Haworth has retired from two highly successful careers and is now embarking on his third as a successful author.

Robert's first career encompassed three decades as a management consultant working with large, complex organizations on major organizational change initiatives. These included implementing new technologies, business processes, and business model improvements. After working for three large global consulting firms, Robert started his own firm and successfully grew it to national prominence over a decade. During this three-decade consulting career, Robert has been inside more companies than he can remember. (This has nothing to do with memory loss, really.) Within these clients, he worked at every level and with all types of people, as he will say, "from the receiving dock to the boardroom."

After selling his company to a British firm, he embarked on his second career as a college professor. He taught the topics that he is passionate about and what he did in the real world, including business management, strategic planning, and entrepreneurship. Robert will tell you that, though he loved his consulting "gig," being in the classroom with his students from all over the world was the highlight of his career. His students must have thought the same because the business school senior class voted Robert their favorite professor year after year.

Now, Robert is beginning his third career as an author. As he will tell you: "When you're running a consulting firm, your days are focused on client management, filling the sales pipeline, hiring and working with your team, and trying to keep one step ahead of competitors. There is no time for reflecting on what you've learned. But when you're in the classroom working with incredible young adults and teaching them important business subjects and telling those amazing stories, well, then you have the time to reflect on what you've learned and, yes, think about the books you want to write."